# About the Author

Carole Golder has been an international astrologer for the past 20 years. She has written several books including *The Seductive Art of Astrology, Love Lives, Moon Signs for Lovers, Carole Golder's Star Signs, Success Through the Stars* and *Your Stars at Work*. Her work has been translated into over 12 languages. She has written for newspapers and magazines all over the world and made many radio and TV appearances. Carole has participated in on-line conferences both in the UK and the US and has given many lectures on astrology — including appearances on five *QE2* cruises! She currently writes an on-line column 'Carole Golder's Love Stars' for AOL. She has many personal clients from every walk of life and on both sides of the Atlantic.

Carole has been living until recently in Massa Lubrense in the South of Italy with her artist partner, Peter Prins. She is currently working on a book about her experiences there, and planning a novel.

# Astrology

# Piatkus Guides

*Other titles in this series include*

A PIATKUS GUIDE

# Astrology

*Carole Golder*

PIATKUS

This book is dedicated to my soulmate, Peter Prins,
whose paintings have inspired me and whose support has
continually encouraged me.

First published in 1999 by
Judy Piatkus (Publishers) Ltd
5 Windmill Street, London W1P 1HF
E-mail: info@piatkus.co.uk

For the latest news and information
on all our titles visit our new website
at www.piatkus.co.uk

**The moral rights of the author have been asserted**

*A catalogue record for this book is available from the British Library*

ISBN 0-7499-2034-3

Set in 12.5/14pt Perpetua
Typeset by Phoenix Photosetting, Chatham
Printed and bound in Great Britain by
Mackays of Chatham PLC

# Contents

# Acknowledgements

I want to thank my friends and clients all over the world, who inspire me to keep on working in the wonderful world of astrology: Adriana and Mario Rispoli for the inspiration I gained from living in their beautiful house in the south of Italy; Air India for making my New York trips so pleasant; and Pasquale Aiello, Maurice Attwood, Bryan Bantry, Frank Clifford, George Golder, Gloria Goldring, Mark Hayles, Fiona Lonsdale and Peter Prins for their support.

# Introduction

I once heard astrology described as the thread on which to hang the story of our lives through our Zodiac signs. This thread has been in existence for more than 5,000 years, ever since the time of the Sumerians, Babylonians, Assyrians and Egyptians, and, at the approach of the next Millennium, it continues to lengthen.

Whether one is a believer or not, there is no doubt that astrology, the art of interpreting the science of astronomy, holds a fascination, if not an ever-growing interest, for a high percentage of the world's population. China, India and the Western world all have their own systems of using astrology in everyday life.

I have been an astrologer for the past 20 years, during which time I have written eight books, a great number of astrology columns and features, and counselled many personal clients on both sides of the Atlantic. For me, astrology is a subject that always teaches something new, and often, when counselling a client, I have learned something important about myself as well.

I became an astrologer almost by accident. While acting as

an agent to many well-known actors and actresses, I met up with the late Patric Walker – one of England's most famous astrologers – who told me that I should become an astrologer myself. I believe there is no such thing as coincidence – this happened at a time when I felt deep down that I wanted to change my life. His look at my chart only served to convince me that the timing was right. I had always had my own, almost sceptical means of checking astrology, often by reading Patric's monthly columns after the event to see if what had been predicted had worked out for me. But it was not long before I was already on the way to believing that astrology perhaps held the answer to many unsolved questions.

As an Aries, I know that I thrive on challenges, and, typical of my sign, I also know when it is time to move on to new pastures. I had been aware of my clairvoyant ability for many years – we *all* have psychic ability but often it lies beneath the surface without being fully developed – and so decided to leave my job as the director of a theatrical agency, and learn more about astrology.

If you feel that the world is changing at such a fast pace that you cannot keep up, especially in the field of modern technology; if you consider yourself emotionally and materially satisfied on many levels, yet are also convinced that there must be something else out there; if you are still searching for a higher knowledge, feeling that deep down you have something more to contribute to the world, but know not how or why – then I hope you will find the answers within these pages.

I have learnt from experience that the way a Pisces thinks is very different from, say, the way a Sagittarius thinks, and that the way you formulate a life plan will depend a great deal on your sign. This will be discussed in Chapter 1, where you will start your personal journey through the Zodiac.

Chapters 2–13 cover each of the individual star signs, and will include such aspects as the effects of your Ruling Planet and your Ascendant and Moon sign, the positive and negative aspects of your sign, how to deal with challenges and obstructions, your star sign meditation to create a better life, use your inner and outer personality to improve your relationships, and career success. Finally, in Chapter 14 I provide a few words of astrological advice for the new Millennium.

Astrology has taught me that we are all born with the ability to make something of ourselves, even if we don't always see how; we all have a contribution to make to the world, whether it is large or small. My aim is to show you how to maximise your potential by capitalising on your positive traits and overcoming your weaknesses. I hope that this book will help you to learn more about yourself, and about everyone with whom you come into contact in your daily life. You will achieve this by reading, not only about your own star sign, but also about each of the 12 signs, because by setting forth on this particular journey through the Zodiac you will discover that you have something to learn from each one.

There is an ever greater need for spirituality in the world, not just as an effort to counter growing violence and materialism, but also because relying on drugs such as Prozac to fight depression is not the answer. Religion no longer seems to provide solace for many people, while psychology and counselling don't always benefit everyone. In addition, many spiritual and self-help books, although extremely useful and uplifting, often address the reader as though we all feel and think in the same way, forgetting about our different star sign personalities.

Over the years my personal experiences have confirmed my belief that the truly successful people in this world are those who have learned to balance their lives emotionally and materially. My intention in this guide to astrology is to show you *all* how to do this successfully.

# 1

# Your Personal Journey Through the Zodiac

Astrology provides a brilliant 12-step programme to a better life. We all have something special to learn from the 12 signs in the great wheel of the Zodiac, and your own journey through the Zodiac can begin with the following suggestions for each star sign's first step along the way:

| | |
|---|---|
| The Aries Step | Coming to terms with the 'me first' syndrome |
| The Taurus Step | Remembering that stubbornness can slow you down |
| The Gemini Step | Trying to follow one path at a time |
| The Cancer Step | Avoiding unnecessary backward steps along the way |
| The Leo Step | Accepting that the leader doesn't always get there first |
| The Virgo Step | Not always worrying where your footsteps lead |
| The Libra Step | Acknowledging that a successful journey involves decisions |

| The Scorpio Step | Realising intensity of purpose doesn't mean tunnel vision |
| The Sagittarius Step | Knowing how and when it's OK to take risks |
| The Capricorn Step | Climbing to success without losing the joy of life |
| The Aquarius Step | Knowing when to toe the line and when to be different |
| The Pisces Step | Following your dreams through to the end of the road |

Do you recognise something about yourself in the above? Perhaps something that you think might have held you back in the past? My most recent book *Your Stars at Work — Using the Power of Astrology to Get Ahead and Get Along on the Job* (Henry Holt, 1997), includes the suggestion that one way to revise your work strategy is to learn more about all the signs. By learning to play a different sign once in a while you can achieve greater success.

On your journey through life it is good to know not just the best way to achieve success, but also the best way to overcome the pitfalls that may occur. Each and every one of us has a destiny to fulfil. Metaphorically, at some moments, the journey through life can be along straight roads that take us to our destination; at other times the path will seem hilly or full of curves, creating limitations we could do without. But the steps on this journey will be made easier if we take advantage of the power of astrology.

This applies to all areas of life, not just work. If you are an impulsive Aries or a sensitive Cancer you will think about things in a different way to a changeable Gemini or an intensely determined Scorpio, while none of you may be able to balance your thoughts in the way that a diplomatic Libra can manage with ease. But all of you can benefit by borrowing some of the positive assets from each other at certain times – Aries will benefit from Libra's ability to weigh things up; Libra will sometimes need an enthusiastic Aries to point out why a particular decision will be extremely beneficial. And, of course, this doesn't apply just to opposite signs: emotionally detached Aquarius will often benefit from a dose of Pisces romanticism. This is why it's so important to read about all the other signs as well as your own, especially if you know that your own natal horoscope contains a mixture of many of them!

Personal relationships will also benefit immensely from a greater understanding of all the star signs. So many relationships between opposite signs, for example Aries and Libra, Taurus and Scorpio, are either highly successful, or else sometimes disastrous. I believe that it is from our opposite sign of the Zodiac that we often have the most to learn, or equally the most to teach; there is something contained within that sign which is lacking in us. Two people of opposite signs can balance their relationship in the most perfect way if they are prepared to accept this fact, but of course, sometimes we all fight against what we know deep down is good for us.

One of the most popular questions asked of an astrologer is the age-old: 'Which sign am I supposed to get on with best?' I truly believe that we actually have the ability to get on with all the signs. It is simply a question of learning more about yourself, including your needs and desires, and then learning more about each of the other 11 signs.

The standard textbook guidelines as to which signs are supposed to get on with each other always say that people born under the same element, i.e. Fire, Earth, Air and Water, are always the most likely to get along well. This means that the Fire signs of Aries, Leo and Sagittarius should always be the best of friends; the Earth signs of Taurus, Virgo and Capricorn will be perfect partners; the Air signs of Gemini, Libra and Aquarius could find no one better than one of their own kind; and the Water signs of Cancer, Scorpio and Pisces were made for one another! Of course sometimes this will be the case, but not always. There are many other factors which go hand in hand to create a good relationship!

Naturally, in any astrology book it is almost impossible not to generalise. In order to be totally accurate and make an in-depth analysis of your personality, it is necessary to draw up a horoscope based on the exact date, time and place of your birth. Many of you reading this book will already know your personal birth charts, either from visiting an astrologer for a consultation, or from having drawn one up using one of the many computer programmes which are in existence today. If you don't, the information contained within these pages will enable you to learn and understand a great deal more about the personality traits of your star sign, and everyone else's. People are often confused because, as the Sun doesn't change signs on the same date every year, but can vary between one or two days, the dates given for each sign are approximate. It becomes even more confusing because books, newspapers and magazines often use slightly different dates. If your birthday falls on 19 February and you find yourself described sometimes as Aquarius, sometimes as Pisces, the only sure way to find out if you were born in the last degree of Aquarius or the first degree of Pisces is to have an astrologer check for you using your exact time, year and place of birth. Astrological charts are calculated using Greenwich Mean Time, which means that time changes between the hemispheres also have to be taken into account.

Another reason for having a chart drawn up for the exact

time and place of your birth is that it will show your Ascendant sign and the position of the Moon and the other planets in your chart. This is your natal chart and tells astrologers a great deal about you and your potential in the years to come.

The Ascendant or Rising sign is the sign that was rising on the Eastern Horizon at the time of your birth. Your Ascendant is considered as important as your Sun and Moon signs because it has a significant influence on the way you live out your life. Many astrologers consider the Ascendant far more important than the Sun sign, which is basically the star sign under which you were born, for example if you were born on 11 January your Sun sign is Capricorn.

I don't necessarily agree with this, although if you were a Capricorn, with a Capricorn Ascendant, you could think of everything you know about your sign, and magnify it! Indeed this would apply to every person, who, to give a very rough guide, was born around 6 a.m., making their Ascendant the same as their Sun sign. A simple do-it-yourself guide to Ascendants is to change it every two hours, for example, using the star sign of Capricorn, at 6 a.m. the Ascendant is Capricorn, but at 8 a.m. the Ascendant is Aquarius, at 10 a.m. Pisces, and so on. This *is* only a rough guide; please check with a professional astrologer or reliable computer astrology program!

Many people are far more like their Sun sign personality than their Ascendant in almost every way. It is important to remember, however, that here again it is hard to generalise. Someone who is born under a certain sign – for example, Taurus – yet has no planet other than the Sun in that sign (Sun in Taurus), and who has very strong aspects between other planets in other star signs, might be a very untypical representative of their Sun sign personality. One planet which is also immensely important in astrology is the Moon, and you can read more about this in one of my earlier books, *Moon Signs for Lovers — An Astrological Guide to Perfect Relationships* (Henry Holt, 1992).

The Moon rules our emotions, and my many years of astrological counselling of clients have shown that you need look no further than the position of the Moon in an individual's chart to gauge the way they behave emotionally. You may have noticed how most Cancerians are affected by the phases of the Moon, especially around Full Moon time, when they are often best left alone to overcome their crabby mood! The Moon rules Cancer, whose element is Water, so it is no surprise to find that its effect is especially strong on this sign.

The Moon's effect on your horoscope will emphasise not only your emotions, but also your innermost needs. The Sun relates to self-expression, the ego and the Father. The Moon represents your instincts, your emotions and the Mother. It is the female side of your nature. Never under-estimate the importance of the Moon in your horoscope. It has a powerful effect on the tides and plants, animals and humans, and its effect on our ability to give and receive love is equally powerful.

The position of the Moon in a horoscope will also enable you to understand why a supposedly impulsive and fiery Aries will sometimes find it difficult to reveal his or her deepest emotions, becoming coldly detached, even in a seemingly ardent love affair. If you discover that the Moon is in the cool and more unemotional Aquarius it will begin to make sense, for the Moon is the emotional *you*.

Saturn, often described as the taskmaster of the Zodiac, is also invariably a major influence in most people's lives. Saturn takes between 28 and 30 years to return to the place that it occupied when you were born, and this 'Saturn return' almost always corresponds to a major time of change in your life, a time that seems to set the pattern for your future. Of course, the position of Saturn in your natal chart will determine how it will affect you, but generally there are very few instances where Saturn has *not* coincided with a turning point in someone's life. Saturn may be a hard taskmaster in some ways, but this planet brings us the greatest rewards in the end, teaching us discipline, and the wisdom to know the difference between what is of transitory and of lasting value.

Astrology is a fascinating subject, even when it is used only in the most general sense. It is a subject which will always have something to teach us, no matter how many years we study it. I think that the best astrologers are those who use their intuitive qualities when developing their craft. We are all born with psychic abilities, but the ever-increasing stresses of the world we live in mean that we tend to let these slip. However, the more you learn about astrology, you will discover that looking at someone's chart is rather like looking at a map of their life. You can see how they came into this world, and the planets and aspects bequeathed to them at birth. And you can see the potential contained within the chart. Astrology is not an exact science; it is the art of interpreting the science of astronomy, but it is an art that once encountered will hold the key to a wonderful journey of self-discovery and success.

As an introduction to astrology, when Patric Walker first looked at my horoscope, he simply drew up a solar chart (a horoscope drawn up for the date that I was born without taking into account my birth time in order to calculate the Ascendant) and then showed the transits of the major planets which were affecting me at that time. This led to my belief that astrology, even in a general sense, can also work to tell us what we are likely to expect in our lives. Of course this means that newspaper astrology should also work in a general sense, and that all astrology columns should correspond in some way. We all know that they don't, which unfortunately tends only to provide ammunition for those who like to point out this fact!

In the following star sign chapters you will learn how to balance your inner and outer personalities. You will also learn more about your Ruling Planet, and how it influences you in your daily life. People seem to be more and more obsessed with how they look on the outside, sometimes turning to a plastic surgeon while they are still in their teens. But if you grow more in touch with your inner personality, nourishing it with greater love and understanding just as you would a little child, you will find that your capacity to give and receive love on the outside will grow stronger too. Your personal journey through the Zodiac will be accomplished with greater ease and with greater success too.

# 2

# Aries
# 21 March – 20 April

If you were born between 21 March and 20 April, you were born under the first sign of the Zodiac, the enthusiastic and energetic, impulsive and ingenuous Aries. The date of 21 March corresponds to the first day of spring. You are a Masculine, Cardinal, Positive sign, the first of the Fire signs; your planetary ruler is Mars, God of War, and the Ram is your planetary symbol. In basic terms, you're the real go-getter of the Zodiac, the sign that faces challenges fearlessly and thrives on a battle – which you often win against all odds.

But it is not wise to race through life with a 'me first' attitude, believing that 'patience' is more of a bore than a virtue. Even an enterprising Aries must learn to realise that there are times when a moment's silence and a chance to step back and rethink can be worth far more than an untimely impetuous onslaught. Of course, there are occasions when your enterprising attitude will bring monumental achievements – who would ever want to undermine your zest for life and your boundless energy? Anyone who has asked a favour of an Aries, no matter how busy that Aries may be, will surely have to admit that it was dealt with almost immediately.

I was fortunate enough to meet the American movie actress, Gloria Swanson, just a few years before she died. We shared the same sign of Aries, and I was talking about impatience and how difficult it is sometimes to contain this quality within our personalities. Gloria said to me, 'I know, because I always want it *now*, not tomorrow, but *now*.' To take this a step further, one of the problems for Aries is that they are sometimes not even satisfied with *now*, but want it *yesterday* – whatever *it* may be.

## *Your Ruling Planet*

An Aries could be forgiven for sometimes treating life as a battlefield, and even for being aggressive. Your ruling planet, Mars, was the Roman God of War, and it is your Martian energy that sometimes encourages you to charge through life rather like an ancient Roman warrior. But it is also this Martian energy which enables you to take the lead fearlessly and to inspire others with your innovative ideas and actions.

The trouble with being a fairly typical Aries is that you rarely know when to stop. It's as though you consider your energy inexhaustible (it certainly exhausts the people around you at times!) and refuse to replenish it even if your inner

voice tells you that you need a break. Maybe you don't actually give yourself the time to listen to your inner voice, considering that rest and relaxation are words which have no
place within your vocabulary.

Mars provides you with your strength and courage, your
passion, sexual drive and your boundless creativity. But Mars
will also accentuate your competitiveness, aggressiveness and
tendency to indulge in temper tantrums when things do not
go your way. It is the influence of Mars that can also make
you accident prone, for you tend to ignore that old maxim
'look before you leap'.

The benefit of learning more about astrology in general,
and particularly about how to accentuate the positive attributes of your sign, is that you *will* find the necessary time to
look deeper within yourself and learn how to harness your
Martian energy. You will learn not to lose your temper or
argue incessantly when things go wrong or take longer than
you expected, but instead you will take a deep breath and
resolve to be more patient.

It is wonderful to have Mars as your ruling planet, for you
will never run short of courage and bravery with which to
deal with the problems or challenges you encounter on your
journey through life. You will always inspire other people
with your enthusiasm and *joie de vivre*, and it is probably true
to say that life with you will rarely be dull. But life does not
have to be a perpetual battlefield – the world will not suddenly stop functioning if Aries takes that little step back and
has a respite from the challenges once in a while.

## Your Ascendant and Moon Sign

As discussed in Chapter 1, in principle you will take on
something of the personality of the sign that was rising when

you were born. If your Ascendant is Aries, remember that the Mars influence will be stronger too.

An Aries with Aries rising will make sure we *all* know that you have leadership potential; with Taurus rising you will have greater patience to wait for tomorrow; with Gemini rising you will need to harness that Martian energy to stick at one thing at a time; while with Cancer rising there will be greater sensitivity in your fiery personality. With Leo rising you need to watch that your strength of character is not combined with too much pride; an Aries with a Virgo Ascendant will have great powers of analysis and discrimination; with Libra rising you will recognise the benefit of seeing both sides of a situation before marching ahead; while with a Scorpio Ascendant you will be even more determined to overcome challenges. With Sagittarius rising you could over-do the risk taking; Capricorn rising means that your material security could take precedence in your life; Aquarius rising brings a humanitarian side to your 'me first' attitude; and, finally, a Pisces Ascendant will make you more sentimental, but hopefully not too impractical.

The Moon in your horoscope highlights both your emotions and your innermost needs. It will naturally have an effect on your star sign personality. As an Aries, with the Moon also in Aries, there will be a vulnerable, idealistic and romantic side to your fiery exterior; a Taurus Moon provides you with a fairly relaxed attitude to dealing with your emotions, holding you back from impulsive moves; a Gemini Moon will accentuate your ability to communicate from the heart, but watch that it doesn't accentuate your headstrong ways as well; while a Cancer Moon will soften even the most hard-hitting and aggressive Aries. A Leo Moon will enhance your determination to make everyone proud of your achievements; a Virgo Moon will sometimes make you question yourself a little too much; the Moon in Libra should help to balance those 'rushing into battle' moods; while the Moon in Scorpio adds determination but sometimes jealousy to your fiery Aries passion. A Sagittarius Moon will highlight your basic Aries enthusiasm for life; a Capricorn Moon helps you to stay the course, giving you greater patience along the way; an Aquarius Moon could tone down your habit of falling in love at the drop of a hat; and, lastly, a Pisces Moon will make you more sensitive and retiring than the other Aries types.

## Accentuate the Positive and Reduce the Negative

Instead of your 'me first' attitude, why don't you try telling yourself to 'think first', before you go racing into something new. If you're typical of the Aries sign, there is always the tendency to start a new project or a new romance enthusiastically without being sure it's what you want deep down. You tend to get bored terribly easily, which is neither good for you nor indeed for anyone else. It's wonderful to be the pioneer of the Zodiac – but even better if you finish what you start!

Remember that patience is a virtue which can be an immense benefit at times. This is not to say that you should sit back and do nothing – as if you could. But a little more of your opposite sign of Libra's ability to balance things will stand you in good stead. Use your energy and courage in a positive way, and always try to take good deep breaths before you argue over something which does not need to be a battle. Don't let your ego take control, but listen carefully to your inner voice, for it is a powerful force.

## Challenges and Obstructions

Try to deal with any challenges and obstructions as calmly as possible. Learn to look at both sides of a situation, and don't get yourself into a panic if you cannot find an immediate resolution. Becoming stressed-out will help no one, including yourself. Remember that Aries rules the head, and you don't want to land yourself with unwanted headaches or migraines just because you're having a trying time.

In many ways you thrive on challenges – they suit your firebrand pioneering personality. You're a real achiever and a positive powerhouse of energy, and the influence of Mars gives you the courage to deal with difficulties in a fearless and enterprising way. But even a battling Aries cannot overcome every problem right away.

Learn to do things at a smoother, steadier pace. Impulsiveness and impatience are far less important than good timing and listening to your intuition. When you truly know what you want out of life, and make the right efforts to achieve this, you will soon find that no challenge or obstruction will seem too great, especially if you find a meditation which will help you to become more calm.

### Your Star Sign Meditation to Help You Create a Better Life

☆ Sit comfortably on the floor in a cross-legged position (or, if this is not comfortable, on a chair).

☆ Close your eyes and visualise a beautiful sunset in front of you. The sun is glowing deep red and you feel its healing and positive energy growing inside you.

☆ Allow your mind to be still, but don't worry if thoughts and ideas insist on coming in – just let them float by like clouds, for all that matters is you and your sunset.

☆ Let yourself sink slowly into a meditative state for approximately 20 minutes, so that you have the time to visualise all the beautiful *after* colours of the sunset, the different shades of reds and rose pinks, and allow them to enter your sub-conscious mind.

Try to perform this meditation twice a day. You will soon start to discover a clarity of vision, a calmness, confidence and realisation of your Aries power, plus an inner knowledge that enables you to make daily decisions in a more positive way and at the same time rise above all the day-to-day problems in your life. You will soon learn instinctively when your 20 minutes are up.

And when you next watch a *real* sunset, remember to wait for that glorious after-glow instead of rushing off in typical Aries fashion! It will prove to you that patience *is* a virtue.

## Balancing Your Inner and Outer Personality to Improve Your Relationships

An Aries client in New York found it the hardest thing in the world to sit back and wait for her new lover to call and arrange the next date. She had always messed up relationships in the past because of her need to be the leader. This was because of her inner vulnerability, a yearning to be loved that few people were allowed to see. By believing more in her inner worth, without the need to become excessively aggressive on the outside, she was able to balance her personality, and her relationships became much easier to sustain.

If you are a typical Aries, the chase and the challenge are wonderfully exciting, but you have a horrible habit of running out of steam once a relationship takes on a more permanent basis. Learn to balance your inner emotional desires with a determination to use your outer strength to work on your relationships so that they can become more fulfilling in every possible way. Fiery passion is highly exciting for a Mars-ruled Aries in the first flush of a new love affair, but you need as much mental stimulation as a Gemini, and plenty of mutual interests if a relationship can be an ongoing delight for years to come.

Affirm to yourself that you will become more patient and understanding, not only with your inner self, but also within your relationships with each and every star sign. This will bring you greater emotional security and happiness along your journey through life.

## A Successful Career

You have the ability to be a high-achieving pioneer because you usually possess masses of drive and vision, plus a forceful and direct style. Your determination to succeed in your chosen career can rarely be faulted. What is much harder for you to accept is that not *every* Aries can be the boss.

You thrive on deadlines, challenges and even power struggles, but the wise Aries will also know that too much stress is self-defeating in the climb to the top. It is important for you to create the right balance between your career and your personal life, so that you can happily unwind at the end of a busy day.

If you *are* in a high-flying position and are typical of your Aries personality, you may have a fear of delegating work, perhaps believing, rightly or wrongly, that no one can do it as well as you. The problem with this attitude is that invariably you take too much upon yourself and create unnecessary stress. The answer is to make sure that you have the right back-up from people on whom you can rely.

If you are determined to become more successful in your career, always remember that a sharp and focused approach, combined with your enthusiasm, energy and enterprising ways, will always bring you the best results. You certainly don't need any lessons in assertiveness, but a few refresher courses in patience and moderation will often help you along the way.

# 3

# Taurus
# 21 April – 20 May

If you were born between 21 April and 20 May, you were born under the second sign of the Zodiac, the practical and persevering, pragmatic and patient Taurus. You are a Feminine, Fixed, Negative sign, the first of the Earth signs; your planetary ruler is Venus, Goddess of Love, and your planetary symbol is the Bull. In basic terms you are the kind of person who can always be depended upon, a loyal and supportive friend, and someone who never seems to get into a panic, even during a crisis.

But whereas Aries, the sign that precedes yours, will sometimes be almost too much of a go-getter, rushing in where angels fear to tread, you will sometimes lag behind, waiting for someone to give you the go-ahead to move on. There is a stubborn side to your personality that ties you to a set routine, even when deep down you know it is time to make some kind of change. It is almost as if, because you're an Earth sign, you feel your feet should be planted firmly on the ground each and every minute of the day. You know you have the ability to succeed at whatever you have set your heart upon, yet sometimes you are unnecessarily scared of taking even the slightest risk in case you jeopardise your security in any way at all.

Taureans are brilliant at juggling a busy career with an equally busy domestic life, and managing to do everything successfully. Indeed, a Taurean client in New York is vice-president of a major company, and also a devoted wife and mother to three small children. And it was Bob, a Taurean screen-writing friend, who inspired me to write my very first book, *Make the Most of Your Sun Sign* (Treasure Press, 1988). He had been joking with someone that he had changed his sign from Taurus to Libra by deed poll. However, even plastic surgery will not alter the fact that the one thing we cannot change about ourselves is our sign – all the more reason for you to make the most of being Taurus!

## *Your Ruling Planet*

Venus, Goddess of Love, is the ruler of Taurus, and underneath your often down-to-earth exterior beats a soft and sensitive heart. Venus bestows you with a love of beauty, a desire for peace and harmony, and a strong sense of refinement and beauty. Her influence as your ruling planet is demonstrated by your interest in art and music, and many of you are extremely creative in these fields.

But there is another side to Venus, which tends to make you place too much emphasis on the more sybaritic side of life, and too little on exerting yourself. There is also an inertia that comes upon many Taureans, often just at those moments when you should have a more get-up-and-go attitude to life. The problem is that if anyone dares tell you this, there is an obstinate look in your eyes, and it's almost as though your feet are pushed down further into the ground. Sometimes you are too concerned with the material side of life, equating security with beautiful possessions and bricks and mortar. And you will not budge from your chosen viewpoint, even when you know deep down that understanding more about your inner self can bring you an easier journey through life.

One benefit of Venus is that she allows you to look on the brighter side of life so that you invariably see the positive side of most situations. You manage to smile sweetly at the world, even when you may be seething inside, for Venus helps to cushion the blow of disappointment. In many ways, the Goddess of Love endows you with immense amounts of romantic idealism, and your sexuality and sensuality are often simmering beneath the surface of a placid personality. But there is also an inner strength combined with self-control and determination that will let you take things at a far slower place than Aries. Rushing headfirst into love is not really your scene – you prefer to allow things to take their time to grow. You search for a tangible commitment within everything, and once you understand that this needs to be found initially within *yourself*, your determination and perseverance will pay handsome dividends.

You share Venus, your ruling planet, with the sign of Libra, and both of you search for friendship and love in your life. Venus adds to your patient, kind and humorous ways, and accentuates your warmth and sensitivity. She will help to make your journey through life a serene and joyful one, provided that you don't stubbornly refuse to change any of the things you *know* you're doing wrong!

## *Your Ascendant and Moon Sign*

As I said earlier, you will take on something of the personality of the sign that was rising when you were born. If your Ascendant is Taurus or Libra, remember that the Venus influence will be stronger too.

As a Taurus with Aries rising you will be less fixed in your ideas, and more enthusiastic about trying out new ones; with Taurus rising you will be doubly dependable and loyal, but perhaps *too* set in your ways; a Gemini Ascendant helps you to become more freethinking and flexible; while Cancer rising highlights your need for emotional and domestic security at all costs. A Leo Ascendant emphasises your determination to achieve success, but could also accentuate those fixed opinions; with Virgo rising you will be brilliantly organised and highly disciplined in just about everything; a Libra Ascendant will highlight your love of beauty and harmony but perhaps a lack of initiative too; while Scorpio rising intensifies the somewhat possessive part of your personality. Sagittarius rising allows you to be more outgoing and adventurous than usual; a Capricorn Ascendant makes you doubly ambitious, but hopefully not doubly materialistic; Aquarius rising adds idealism to material hopes and desires; and, finally, a Pisces Ascendant combines your practical ways with perhaps a little *too* much sensitivity!

The Moon in your horoscope highlights both your emotions and your innermost needs. It will naturally have an effect on your star sign personality. As a Taurus with the Moon in Aries you will have a fiery and outgoing approach to life; a Taurus Moon will highlight your desire for emotional stability; a Gemini Moon will accentuate a need for mental stimulation; while a Cancer Moon enhances your desire for security on every level. A Leo Moon brings deep inner strength but also a need for attention; a Virgo Moon highlights the Earth qualities of your sign and the amount of work you put into *everything* in your life; a Libra Moon accentuates the Venusian qualities of your sign — peace, beauty and harmony at all costs; and the Moon in Scorpio emphasises your sensuality and makes you fairly invincible in achieving your objectives. A Sagittarius Moon allows you to be more outgoing and happy-go-lucky, and less fixed in your objectives; a Capricorn Moon highlights your pragmatic approach and could make you almost too serious about life; the Moon in Aquarius makes you more detached emotionally, and probably more unpredictable; and in Pisces the Moon will enhance your innermost desires for romantic life, but could make you more impractical.

## Accentuate the Positive and Reduce the Negative

You are immensely patient, kind and loyal, but if you really want to be more successful in your journey through life, it would often help you to move a little faster. The fact that you're an Earth sign really doesn't have to mean that your feet are planted (metaphorically *and* literally) on the ground every single day!

It may be your love of creature comforts that contributes to your fear of change, but you don't have to stick to the same routine all your life, especially if you feel you're losing out on certain things. Try to become more flexible in your everyday life, and always make the best possible use of your creative and artistic talents. Very few Taureans have neither the ability nor the determination to achieve their objectives. Refuse to be held back by being unnecessarily fixed in your ideas and opinions, or by putting all your material needs before what you yearn for deep inside. Remember that every sign has something to learn from its opposite sign in the Zodiac. Yours is the invincible Scorpio – and you can be just as invincible!

## Challenges and Obstructions

You're usually extremely good at dealing with any challenges and obstructions, invariably because you are willing to sit them out with a patient and persistent attitude. But this does not mean that you should bury your head in the sand, ostrich fashion, and simply ignore any problems that come your way, for that could create greater problems in the long term.

If you're typical of your sign, you do not like arguments, especially with raised voices and angry gestures. Your anger is slow to burn and you will be more successful when you try to resolve differences of opinion in a calm and practical way.

But remember that you can also alienate other people by being excessively fixed in your opinions, and stubborn and unyielding in the way that you deal with things. Your famous stubbornness may be born of an inner fear of losing your grasp of a situation, but a wise Taurean will have the faith to understand that sometimes it is necessary to let go in order to move ahead. No challenge or obstruction will be too great for you, especially if you have a meditation to enable you to be closer to the Inner You.

## YOUR STAR SIGN MEDITATION TO HELP YOU CREATE A BETTER LIFE

☆ Choose a quiet place where you will not be disturbed.

☆ Sit comfortably on the floor in a cross-legged position (or on a chair if this feels easier for you).

☆ Close your eyes and imagine that you are listening to a favourite piece of music.

☆ Visualise yourself sitting in a beautiful meadow, with trees around that are stretching upwards and outwards towards a clear blue sky.

☆ The scent of flowers is all around you; imagine yourself breathing it in.

☆ Be aware of the rays of energy shooting out from your heart into the heavens above, and surrender your material desires to the beauty of nature, allowing the strength and energy of the earth to revitalise your own body.

☆ Let yourself sink into this meditative state for about 20 minutes.

☆ Then allow yourself to become more aware of the energising life force within you, and of your ability to rise above any difficulties you face in life with a grounded yet more flexible attitude.

Try to perform this meditation twice a day, and you will soon know instinctively when your 20 minutes are up. The next time you are in the countryside or in a garden, look around you at the many different shades of green, and remember to let the colours and scents soak deep into your inner being. They will add to your feeling of inner peace and stability.

## Balancing Your Inner and Outer Personality to Improve Your Relationships

More Taureans seem to be settled in happy and stable relationships than almost any other sign, so you are obviously doing a lot that is right! For those of you who do feel that you are lacking something in your emotional life, perhaps you are sometimes guilty of taking too long to let your feelings show. You should not necessarily rush up to the object of your affections and declare everlasting love after the very first date, even if you *are* ruled by the Goddess of Love and possess an earthy sexuality which can be irresistible! But sometimes it is also very hard to know just what you *do* feel, even after a significant time, although you are brilliant at creating strategies to get to know someone reasonably well.

In order to successfully balance your inner and your outer personality, always remember that while material security is extremely important to the Outer You, the security of a committed, long-lasting and sexually fulfilling emotional relationship is paramount in the desires of your Inner Self. It is also necessary for you to accept that if a relationship has truly run its course, you may do yourself more harm than good by trying to stubbornly hang on, especially once you have done everything within your power to help resolve any problems.

You are someone with your feet set very firmly upon the ground in most areas of your life, yet it is sometimes surprising to discover that you are not always as emotionally secure as you appear on the surface. When you learn to trust your Inner Self with greater confidence, you will soon be able to balance your emotional desires with your material needs and enjoy the perfect partnerships that you deserve.

## A Successful Career

At the risk of offending a few Taureans, it must be said that you do not always appear to be as outwardly motivated in your attempts to climb the ladder of success as you may feel deep within. A step-by-step long-term approach to achieving success, together with your undoubtedly persistent efforts to fulfil your potential, are all very well, but there are times when you may need to be more of a dynamo and to demonstrate your talents with greater flair and even a touch more originality.

You are so well organised and methodical in your working practices, that it's no wonder that anyone who has a Taurean colleague feels lost if they are out of the office even for a day. However, the fixed aspect of your earthy Taurus personality can sometimes make you stubborn and obstinate at the very moments you should be more open to advice and suggestions. If you want to be a high flyer in today's technological world you must continually be up to date with what is happening on every level, which can sometimes mean changing your own tried and true methods of doing things.

Feel comfortable by all means, but don't ever give yourself too long to achieve your hoped-for goals unless you want someone else to pip you at the post.

# 4

# Gemini
# 21 May – 20 June

If you were born between 21 May and 20 June, you were
born under the third sign of the Zodiac, the fun-loving and
frolicsome, intelligent and often intellectual Gemini. You are
a Masculine, Mutable, Positive sign, and the first of the Air
signs; your planetary ruler is Mercury, Winged Messenger of
the Gods, and your planetary symbol is the Twins. This duality within your personality can make you changeable in your
moods, but never dull! You're insatiably curious about the
knowledge that life has to offer, and are always searching for
something new. But make sure you don't wear yourself out
by trying to do too many things at once; Gemini rules the

nervous system, and it is not wise to over-stress yourself.

Mental stimulation is extremely important to anyone born under the sign of Gemini, and you are definitely not someone who could suffer fools gladly. In one of my earlier books, *Carole Golder's Star Signs* (Henry Holt, 1994), the importance of getting in touch with the Inner You was emphasised. Don't just be curious about other people and how *they* live their lives; learn to understand who *you* are, and why you are the way you are. Sometimes you are so busy rushing from one thing to another that you almost exhaust the rest of us just telling us about everything you have planned for your day.

With excellent powers of communication and reason, plus an abundance of versatility, it is not surprising that you can become extremely successful. Many Geminis manage to be creative in more than one field. One of my good friends, Simon Callow, excels at writing, acting *and* directing, and is a perfect example of a Gemini who has learned to harness those Gemini reins and to fulfil his artistic potential. But other Geminis scatter your talents far too wide and always seem to have an abundance of unfulfilled aspirations, probably because you're too busy to be organised!

It may be fairly difficult for a Gemini to concentrate on only one thing at a time, because your mind seems to move ahead extremely fast. When you become more in touch with your Inner Self, you will soon appreciate the benefit of those moments of calm when your mind becomes still.

## Your Ruling Planet

Your ruling planet, Mercury, is the planet of communication, so it's hardly surprising that you are able to talk nineteen to the dozen at all hours of the day or night, bowling the rest of us over with your mental ability and nervous energy. Mercury is the fastest moving of all the planets, so perhaps it is also no surprise that your journey through life is often conducted in such a rapid way.

Mercury's influence helps you to master foreign languages and the latest computer technology. In mythology Mercury was known as the Winged Messenger of the Gods, and your intellectual prowess and ability to produce innovative ideas are certainly given a boost by having Mercury as your planetary ruler.

Your communicative skills are almost unsurpassed, but you sometimes come across as being far more of a 'thinking' than a 'feeling' person. This may be fine in certain areas, but can create problems when you do need to reveal your deepest feelings, or to empathise with someone else. You possess lots of intuition, so perhaps it's just another instance of learning to be more in touch with your inner being, and not trying to deal with everything in a purely intellectual way.

It is wonderful to have Mercury as your ruling planet, for it means you will never be at a loss for words! It also means you have the ability to be one of those sparkling personalities everyone loves to be around. But before you get too carried away with the good news, you should also be aware that some of you are accused of having a Dr Jekyll and Mr Hyde personality, or are described as being 'two faced' and even 'schizophrenic'.

It is up to you to ensure that your nervous energy is kept at bay so that you don't feel the need to wave your hands and arms around quite so much. It's exhausting for us to watch you, so it must be exhausting for you as well! Use the power of Mercury to communicate with *yourself* – tell yourself that it's time to channel your energies in a better way and to become more focused on the matters in hand. You will soon discover that you become even more effective in communication once you have learned to balance yourself on mind, body and soul level, and it's not as hard as you might think.

## Your Ascendant and Moon Sign

You will, in principle, take on something of the personality of the sign that was rising when you were born. If your Ascendant is Gemini, remember that the Mercury influence will be stronger too.

As a Gemini with Aries rising you must really learn to follow through on ideas; Taurus rising means you have greater ability to remain focused; a Gemini Ascendant highlights the need to organise yourself brilliantly; while Cancer on the Ascendant highlights your emotions on a deeper level. Leo rising means you will want to prove your star quality to all; Virgo on the Ascendant gives you a double dose of Mercury's influence and enables you to be extremely analytical; Libra rising makes you fair-minded but perhaps a little indecisive; while a Scorpio Ascendant gives you an intense determination to prove yourself invincible. Sagittarius rising could make you a little carelessly optimistic about taking on too much; a Capricorn Ascendant will make you one of the hardest-working Gemini folks around; Aquarius rising will make you even more intellectual but also more unpredictable; and, finally, a Pisces Ascendant will certainly heighten your sensitivity and open up your emotional side.

The Moon in your horoscope highlights both your emotions and your innermost needs. It will naturally have an effect on your star sign personality. As a Gemini with an Aries Moon you could be passionate but a little too flirtatious; with a Taurus Moon you will feel far more down-to-earth and settled in your emotions; a Gemini Moon highlights your instincts and your intuitions, but also your tendency to flit around; while the Moon in Cancer brings out a domestic- ated and more sensitive side of your butterfly personality. A Leo Moon makes you determined to be noticed and adored; the Moon in Virgo heightens your need for mental com- munication at all costs and makes you very critical too; a Libra Moon could help to convince you that good partner- ships are better than playing the field; and a Scorpio Moon will make you more intense and emotional than most people born under your sign. A Sagittarius Moon could almost make you even *more* of a freedom loving soul; a Capricorn Moon will put your feet firmly on the ground; in Aquarius the Moon will mean you need to work harder at expressing those really deep emotions; and, finally, a Pisces Moon could have you yearning for a bit more sentimentality in your life.

## Accentuate the Positive and Reduce the Negative

It would be pointless to tell you to think before you speak, because if you're a typical Gemini you never *stop* thinking or mentally searching for more variety in your life! But in order to make the most of your many talents and abilities in a truly positive way, why not devote half an hour each morning to just sitting still and clearing your mind. Then begin to organ- ise your thoughts and divide a blank sheet of paper into three columns. The first column will contain all that you hope to achieve, the second will show your current involvements, and the third will consist of everything you are prepared to put on hold in order to concentrate on your most important objectives. Naturally you can do all this on a computer, but the very act of writing it all down is good discipline for a restless mind such as yours.

The negative aspects of your personality, at least the ones which other people seem to accuse you of possessing, tend to be an overly superficial view of people and things, plus the tendency to be somewhat fickle and flirtatious when love comes around. Personally, I don't think I've met many people born under your sign who can put up with too much routine for long, yet there are bound to be occasions when *some* kind of routine will benefit you immensely.

## Challenges and Obstructions

Challenges that are mentally stimulating will always fire your imagination and inspire you to be as pioneering and enthusiastic as any of the Fire signs. The problem is getting you to follow through until the end! It is also sometimes easier for you to mentally detach yourself from any humdrum challenges and obstructions than to search constructively for a solution. A certain amount of mental detachment is fine, but too much will rarely enable you to overcome the initial problems, and is hardly going to benefit you in the long run, so a change of attitude will be necessary.

Never let yourself be more preoccupied with your *ideas* about a situation than with the situation itself. The positive side of your character enables you to see many sides of a subject, but you're not always prepared to listen to advice when it is given, preferring to persevere with your own theories.

If you encounter difficulties because you have too many occupations or projects in the pipeline at the same time, then resolve once and for all to change your *modus operandi*. One way will be to find a meditation that will calm your active mind and enable you to see the way ahead more clearly.

## YOUR STAR SIGN MEDITATION TO HELP YOU CREATE A BETTER LIFE

☆ Sit comfortably on the floor in a cross-legged position (or, if this not comfortable, on a chair).

☆ Close your eyes and visualise a white dove soaring in the air above you – a dove of peace, spreading harmony on the earth below. There may be some other smaller birds following it, but allow your mind to slowly still itself, and concentrate on the one white dove. Don't worry if thoughts insist on coming in – think of them as being like the smaller birds and let them go on by.

☆ Allow yourself to sink slowly into a meditative state for approximately 20 minutes so that you have time to let your Gemini restlessness disappear into the ether, and your mind becomes calm and still.

Try to perform this meditation twice a day. Once you have done this a few times you will soon know when the 20 minutes is up. You will discover that your mind is less restless, and your concentration will be greater. Your journey through life will be a whole lot smoother too. And the next time you look up at the sky and see some birds flying by joyously, remember the white dove of peace, and think of your own life as being equally joyous and free.

## Balancing Your Inner and Outer Personality to Improve Your Relationships

Not all Gemini men and women deserve the title of 'social butterfly' of the Zodiac, although this has been bestowed upon some of you more than once! Many of you have perfectly happy and fulfilling relationships that last throughout your lives. But you also demand a never-ending supply of mental stimulation from a partner, perhaps because the idea of total commitment is also daunting to you.

The duality of your sign of the Twins, combined with your mercurial mind, often seems to make it difficult for you to stand still and reflect. When and if you do, it's as though you refuse to look towards your Inner Self to ask what you need to create a more fulfilling life. Deep down you may yearn for a soulmate, yet you may also behave thoughtlessly at times towards the people you care for most. Remember that relationships need to be worked at if they are to grow stronger. Try harder to understand the deepest needs and desires of other people, and don't search for an escape route the moment you feel slightly bored by someone's conversation.

Be more in touch with every aspect of your inner being. Affirm to yourself that you will try to lose your outward restlessness, and channel your mind into positive attributes so that relationships can bring you even greater satisfaction in the coming years. When your mind is calm and your heart is open you will discover much greater emotional security and contentment during your journey through life.

## A Successful Career

In one of my earlier books, *Success Through the Stars* (Henry Holt, 1996), I quoted a maxim that is often applied to

Geminis: 'I think, therefore I am'. If you want to be more successful in your career, it is essential for you to say 'I think, therefore I do'. All too often you have many brilliant ideas whirling around in your mind, but you lack the necessary determination to put them into action.

If you have too many projects in the pipeline at the same time it is inevitable that one or more of them will suffer. Resolve to concentrate on one thing at a time, and learn to appreciate the value of writing out that daily schedule. The benefits will be immense because a truly successful Gemini is one who knows how to focus. Channelling your mind and your energy on to something you find mentally stimulating will be a great bonus. But obviously there will be times when you find yourself having to do a fairly boring task. Unfortunately that is part and parcel of most people's working lives; once you apply yourself conscientiously to dealing with it, you will soon be able to move on to something else.

If you're truly determined to become more successful in your career, always remember that you *are* the sign of communication and that you are also extremely perceptive and receptive to what is going on around you. With masses of idealism and talent at your fingertips, all you really need is a little more concentration and organisation to propel you further up the ladder of success!

# 5

# Cancer
# 21 June – 21 July

If you were born between 21 June and 21 July, then you were born under the fourth sign of the Zodiac, the sensitive and sentimental, caring and compassionate Cancer. You are a Feminine, Cardinal, Negative sign, and the first of the Water signs; your planetary ruler is the Moon, and the Crab is your planetary symbol. Rather like a crab itself, you are hard-shelled on the surface and soft-centred underneath.

Whereas Gemini is a thinker, you are definitely a *feeler*, and you draw things toward you on a deeply personal level. You will empathise with others, are strongly self-protective (although sometimes unfairly accused of being self-centred too), and are able to attune yourself psychically to what is going on around you. Although you are often referred to as the most domesticated sign in the whole Zodiac, there is also a deeply ambitious side to your nature, and certainly a tenacious one when it comes to achieving your objectives.

There is also a tendency within your personality to cling on far too long to people or possessions that have run their course in your life. Sentimentality is worthy, provided you do not take it to extremes. Sometimes you block yourself from moving ahead in a hoped for direction because you are anchored all too firmly in the past. I can think of more than a few Cancerian friends and clients who have hung on to negative emotional relationships because of a fear of being left alone. Considering that you are one of the most intuitive of all the signs, you must draw on this intuition to help yourself more, especially as you possess an inner strength which is to be admired!

Never let anyone have an opportunity to accuse you of being too much like your symbol, the Crab, by clinging to people when they may need to feel free. It is important for you to stand on your own two feet and not scuttle around in someone else's shadow.

If you're typical of your sign, you have a great sense of humour, and this will always be a big asset in your journey through life, especially if you learn to laugh at yourself a little more!

## Your Ruling Planet

Your ruling planet is the Moon, which governs the tides of the sea and influences you at the very soul of your being. No matter where this planetary ruler was placed in your chart when you were born, it will have a profound effect on your emotions. The Sun relates to your ego, but the Moon relates to your emotions, and also to your unconscious state, your instincts and your habits. The Moon will help to make you receptive to your deepest feelings, and will enhance your feminine, maternal and nurturing instincts, and also adds to your inborn ability to heal other people. In men, this feminine part of your personality is not negating your masculinity – it will merely sharpen your instincts and feelings in a positive way! This planetary ruler also gives Cancerians an extremely retentive memory and heightens your sensitivity and intuition.

In one of my earlier books, *Moon Signs for Lovers* (Henry Holt, 1992), I wrote extensively about the Moon's effect on relationships and your romantic life in general. With the Moon as your very own planetary ruler you will have a wonderful source of strength to enable you to learn more about the Inner You, and to understand at the deepest possible level a great deal more about your vulnerability and emotional needs.

It is important to try and take notice of the actual phases of the Moon, or at least to make sure you know when there is a New or Full Moon. This is because it affects your mood swings in much the same way as it affects the tidal ebb and flow of the sea. Haven't you often noticed that you seem to feel more energised at New Moon time? Or perhaps moody or depressed when the Full Moon comes round again? Think about it next time you feel your moods are changing, and always try to begin new projects around the New Moon when your creativity is usually very high.

The sensitivity bequeathed upon you by the Moon is a special gift indeed provided you use it in a positive way. It is when this sensitivity becomes 'ultrasensitivity' that you create problems. Never allow yourself to get locked inside your emotions to such an extent that you fail to see the bigger picture in the world outside. Let the Moon's power inspire you to listen silently to your inner voice and then to listen to its advice to fulfil your outer needs.

## Your Ascendant and Moon Sign

In principle, you will take on something of the personality of the sign that was rising when you were born. If your Ascendant is Cancer, remember that the Cancerian influence will be stronger too, as will the influence of your ruler, the Moon.

A Cancer with Aries rising makes you more enterprising and outgoing; while a Taurus Ascendant will make you work harder, but hopefully will not make you stubborn and changeable! A Gemini Ascendant will combine your ability to feel things instinctively with a creative thought pattern; while a Cancer Ascendant means you will be doubly sensitive and intuitive, but hopefully not too moody! Leo rising helps you to have greater self-confidence in yourself and your aspirations; while a Virgo Ascendant gives you greater powers of analysis, but keep any worrying in check. A Libra Ascendant adds to your charm and helps you to see both sides of situations, but make sure you don't become laid-back; Scorpio rising highlights your emotional nature, and the need to be alone if you're feeling a bit down; while a Sagittarius Ascendant helps you overcome those mood swings and have an optimistic view of life. Capricorn rising means your opposite sign has something to teach you, and you will work really hard to achieve your objectives; and with an Aquarius Ascendant you could be much more unconventional than your fellow Cancerians. Finally, a Pisces Ascendant means a double dose of the Water element – so don't be too romantic or impractical.

The Moon in your horoscope highlights your emotions and your innermost needs, and as your very own planetary ruler, it will naturally have an effect on your star sign personality. An Aries Moon will make your emotions more passionate and you will soon overcome any down moods; a Taurus Moon will make you even more determined for tender loving care; while a Gemini Moon will take away your tendency to cling on to people and make you more independent. A Cancer Moon will accentuate *everything* about your Cancerian personality, but try not to wallow in your emotions! The Moon in Leo will give you lots of pride but could make you fairly demanding too; with a Scorpio Moon you'll be incredibly intense about your emotions and perhaps overly possessive too; a Sagittarius Moon will make you more freedom loving than many Cancerians; and a Capricorn Moon provides you with a strong need for security, and a liking for tradition. An Aquarius Moon enables you to detach yourself more easily from your emotions; and, last but not least, a Pisces Moon will probably enhance how you feel and what you yearn for in your life.

## Accentuate the Positive and Reduce the Negative

If you're a typical Cancerian, I know that sometimes it can be hard for you to avoid those upswings of moods (especially around Full Moon time) which can turn you from a gentle and amusing person into someone rather miserable. I don't expect anyone to be bright and outgoing every day, but I've occasionally wondered if you secretly rather enjoy the sympathy you receive from others when you admit you're feeling rather down. Perhaps you don't realise that your star sign has a fantastic sense of humour — so resolve to use it more.

Take a tip from Sagittarius and try to be more optimistic about life, and don't shrink back into your Cancerian shell if you have to cope with a few knocks along the way. Never be too clinging with people, especially when you know deep down that they really need to be free. I know this can be a problem with Cancerian parents who worry about their children leaving the security of the family home. But always remember that you had to do the same thing once!

Remember to balance your aspirations and ideals with acquiring greater self-knowledge – you will soon discover even more positive moments in your journey through life.

## Challenges and Obstructions

Try to deal with any challenges and obstructions in a calm and philosophical way, and never crawl back into your shell rather than face up to things. Don't work yourself up into a depressed state or become so self-protective that you think the whole world is against you, and that the tricky problem you're facing was only put there for you. Anyone who has ever had anything to do with a Cancerian knows that you are ultra-sensitive at times, but *you* know that underneath you can be quite a tough cookie too.

Once you have learned to find a greater sense of security within yourself, the knowledge that you have the ability to overcome most problems will be a saving grace, and you will find yourself becoming more optimistic along the way.

Believe in the power of your intuition – remember that you often sense difficulties before they even arise, and think what an amazing advantage *that* can be, especially as that will enable you to make the right moves at the perfect time. You will also benefit from a meditation that allows you to still your mind and allow your instincts to flow through.

## Your Star Sign Meditation to Help You Create a Better Life

☆ Sit comfortably on the floor in a cross-legged position (or, if this is not comfortable, on a chair).

☆ Close your eyes and visualise yourself sitting on a beautiful beach in the moonlight, with the sound of the waves breaking gently on the sand.

☆ Imagine that the light of the silvery moon above you is bathing you in its reflected glow and helping you to release any pressures or emotional problems you are holding within you.

☆ Allow your mind to be still, but don't worry if thoughts and ideas do insist on coming in – just let them float by as though the pressures or problems are floating by alongside them.

☆ Let yourself sink slowly into a meditative state for approximately 20 minutes, so that you have the benefit of the rays of the Moon wafting over you enhancing you with added intuition and perception.

Try to perform this meditation twice a day. You will soon start to discover clarity of vision, a calmness, confidence and realisation of your Cancer power, plus an inner knowledge that enables you to make your daily decisions in a more positive way, and at the same time to rise above any day-to-day problems.

And when you next see a New Moon, remember that it will give you not only increased energy and optimism, but also a more perceptive view of life as well.

## Balancing Your Inner and Outer Personality to Improve Your Relationships

Emotional needs and desires are perhaps more important to a Cancerian than almost any of the other signs. I have counselled many Cancerian clients who are always yearning for the perfect relationship, but I have often found that sometimes the absence of a long-standing emotional tie has been partly their fault.

If you're typical of your sign, you almost seem to wear your heart on your sleeve and this can frighten off the very person you're hoping to attract. In order to balance your inner and outer personality, you must avoid allowing your mood swings to control you, or being too clinging with anyone just because you fear the thought of being on your own. There is a tendency in most Cancerians to nurture and protect the ones they love, but very few people embarking on a relationship want to feel overly protected as this soon starts to feel like being possessed.

Learn to let go of whatever past emotional baggage you've been holding onto deep inside you, including all those unnecessary fears and insecurities. In this way you will be free to move on with a more positive attitude. When you start to have a better relationship with your own inner being on a mind, body and spirit level, you will find yourself much more successful at having a good relationship with a perfect partner. And always remember that with the Moon ruling the emotional side of your life, your instincts and intuitions will be a powerful asset during your journey through life.

## A Successful Career

Anyone who thinks that you're much too emotional and interested in your domestic life ever to make of a success of a career must think again!

If you are longing to become more successful in your career and feel you've become stuck in a rut, get rid of self-doubt and indecision and vow that you will make the most of your talents and abilities from now on. Always remember to listen to your intuition when you're planning your work strategies, and try never to display signs of jealousy or moodiness if a colleague achieves more success than you do.

Endeavour to work in a field that really interests you and is not simply a dead-end job. As a Cardinal sign you are full of enterprising qualities, and even though you may be content to sit back and take orders for a while, it certainly won't be long before your brilliant memory and ability to adapt to your environment will enable you to go full steam ahead.

Just like your opposite sign of Capricorn, you are often extremely ambitious and are prepared to put in long hours to fulfil your maximum potential. Career success for you goes hand in hand with financial success, creating security not just for you but for your loved ones too. Your instinct and ambition will help you to achieve both.

# 6

# Leo
# 22 July – 21 August

If you were born between 22 July and 21 August, you were born under the fifth sign of the Zodiac, the creative and charismatic, lovable and larger-than-life Leo. You are a Masculine, Fixed, Positive sign, the second of the Fire signs; your planetary ruler is the Sun, and the Lion is your planetary symbol. In basic terms, you're often proud, dynamic and ambitious, yet with a hidden vulnerability and innocence. You're like a small child who smiles joyfully when the sun shines, but cries when the rain is teeming down.

If you are a typical Leo, you have an inborn ability to see the positive side of life, even if you are sometimes a little *too* extrovert and extravagant in your ways! It may also be difficult for you to accept anything less than first place. Your excuse will be that, as Leo the Lion, you're the king of the jungle and the regal ruler of the Zodiac. However, if you want to enjoy a smooth journey through life, it is wise to accept second place on occasion, and to avoid being unduly bossy or domineering even if you do think you always have the right to give the orders. As a Fixed sign, there are times when you can be almost as stubborn and obstinate as Taurus.

Leo rules the heart, and you really are one of those people who do almost everything from your heart, with a sunny and sparkling personality that makes it a pleasure to be around you. The fifth house of the Zodiac relates to love affairs, creativity and children. You're at your best when your emotional and creative feelings are fulfilled. But try not to demand love as your due, or expect constant praise for your efforts. Sometimes you need to be more in touch with your inner being and learn to love this more – then you will become more secure emotionally and less reliant on other people's heartfelt outpourings of praise.

If you're a typical Leo, you have enormous bursts of energy, followed by periods of indolence when you become extremely upset if anyone dares to call you lazy. You're not always very good at balancing these two sides of your personality, and you could become even more successful if you learn to organise yourself a little better.

## Your Ruling Planet

With the powerful Sun, which is such a vital cosmic force, as your ruling planet, it's hardly surprising that you are such a bright and shining personality (most of the time that is). The

Sun highlights your natural warmth and your passionate and enthusiastic zest for life, although at the same time it can enhance your desire for admiration, too. Throughout the centuries Sun worship existed as a religious tradition; in mythology, the Greeks Apollo, Dionysus and Hermes were all said to be descendants of the Sun. We have had many Sun Goddesses throughout the ages too, and more than a few Leo men and women thrive on adulation today, even if they don't expect us to worship them!

It's fantastic to have the Sun as your ruling planet because its powerful energy gives you increased determination to be extremely successful in your chosen field. The Sun adds to your dynamic and creative flair, and highlights your sparkling and often flamboyant personality. It adds to your image and sense of identity, and enables you to stand out in a crowd in your inimitable larger-than-life way, thus demonstrating your ability to be a real star. But it is important to use the positive powers of this planet for your highest good, so don't allow yourself to become too extrovert, power crazy or vain. Remember that, although it may not always be apparent, sometimes even a Leo needs to wait in the wings and let another sign demonstrate his or her own star quality.

It can be no coincidence that many Leo men and women are sun worshippers when they go on holiday – but please don't be such a worshipper of your ruling planet that you create the threat of problems with your health.

Another wonderful aspect of having the Sun as your very own planetary ruler is that it gives you such a positive outlook on life. You invariably have the ability to look on the bright side of things, to see that proverbial glass of water as half full instead of half empty. I consider myself fortunate in having Peter Prins as my extremely positive and creative Leo partner, because if you're a typical Leo you are also one of the most supportive signs around — provided we praise you for being so of course.

## Your Ascendant and Moon Sign

You will almost certainly take on something of the personality of the sign that was rising when you were born. If your Ascendant is Leo, the influence of the Sun will be even stronger too.

As a Leo with Aries rising you will have greater fiery strength, but could be overly impatient and bossy; a Taurus Ascendant brings greater staying power to achieve your objectives, but could mean you're also more stubborn; Gemini rising adds to your creative flair and increases your confidence to talk your way to greater success; while a Cancer Ascendant makes you less extrovert and more sensitive. Leo with Leo rising highlights your endearing qualities of a loveable Lion, but could also make you *much* too bossy; Virgo rising could make even you critical of those larger-than-life ways, but in a positive sense; Libra rising adds the need for peace and harmony within your life; while Scorpio rising tones down your extrovert side and makes you more secretive, but equally determined to be a star! A Sagittarius Ascendant accentuates your positive qualities, but could also make you overly careless and outspoken; a Capricorn Ascendant makes you more conservative in your overall view of life and less in need of the glamour and glitter; Aquarius rising highlights your creative flair but will make you more unpredictable; and, finally, Pisces rising accentuates your romantic desires and your inborn sensitivity.

The Moon in your horoscope highlights both your emotions and your innermost needs. It will naturally have an effect on your star sign personality. As a Leo, with the Moon in Aries you will be doubly passionate about love and your innermost needs; a Taurus Moon could make you somewhat stubborn emotionally and perhaps a little lazy too; a Gemini Moon will mean you want love, praise and masses of mental stimulation – so make sure you also provide them for others too; and a Cancer Moon adds a soft and sensitive quality to the extrovert you. The Moon in Leo gives you positive inner emotions and masses of idealism; a Virgo Moon has you analysing some of your innermost needs in a realistic way; a Libra Moon will make you appreciate the importance of greater balance for the Inner *and* the Outer You; while a Scorpio Moon accentuates your emotional desires and needs in a more burning and intense way. A Sagittarius Moon highlights your need to be more in touch with that Inner You; a Capricorn Moon adds a practical side to your emotions; an Aquarius Moon means you might find it harder to reveal your deepest feelings, even to yourself; and, lastly, a Pisces Moon will make you even more romantic, sweet and lovable – but perhaps more impractical.

## Accentuate the Positive and Reduce the Negative

If you're a typical Leo you might resent the very suggestion that you possess any negative aspects. Perhaps that is because your planetary symbol, the Lion, is recognised as the king of the jungle, which rules over all the other animals, and you in turn seem to feel you take precedence over all of us! But never be patronising and over-powering, even if we don't immediately recognise that you're a real star.

You are one of the most sparkling, generous and warmhearted signs in the Zodiac. You're also great fun to be with and have a much appreciated ability to throw a little sweetness and light our way. It is rarely obvious at the onset that you have quite a dictatorial side too, but once you have learned to tone down any tendency to be domineering or to take over as 'the star of the show' you will have a much smoother journey through life. Some Leos are a little too concerned about having an audience of friends or colleagues who will constantly praise you for your efforts; Leo women are especially guilty of this. Learn to have greater faith in your own ability to judge your efforts, and never be lazy in your efforts to achieve the success you deserve.

## Challenges and Obstructions

You are basically such a positive individual that it is really frustrating for you when you come up against difficult situations. One Leo tendency is simply to roar like a lion, while another is to fall dejectedly into a 'feeling sorry for yourself' state, especially if you feel that your pride has been affronted.

The best way for you to deal with any challenges and obstructions is to listen to your inner voice, that little child within you, rather than to your ego, because the Leo ego can interfere with the rational and logical way of dealing with things. Your inner voice will enable you to calmly listen to your instincts and to have greater belief in your power to rise above difficulties.

One way to become more in touch with your inner being is to find a meditation which suits you, and which will help you to become cool, calm and collected so that you can deal with challenges with greater ease.

### YOUR STAR SIGN MEDITATION TO HELP YOU CREATE A BETTER LIFE

☆ Sit comfortably on the floor in a cross-legged position (or, if this is not comfortable, on a chair).

☆ Close your eyes and visualise yourself sitting in the middle of a field filled with thousands of bright golden sunflowers. Take in their beauty, and feel the warmth from their deep yellow gold colour filling your body from the crown of your head to your heart.

☆ Allow your mind to be still, but don't worry if thoughts and ideas insist on coming in – just let them float by like petals from the flowers, for all that matters is you and the energy flowing into your body from the sunflowers and the sun shining down upon them.

☆ Let yourself sink slowly into a meditative state for approximately 20 minutes so that when you do open your eyes you will feel energised and even more positive and dynamic in your thoughts and actions.

This meditation will allow you to gain an inner knowledge of yourself that will help you to rise above any problems in your daily life with greater strength of purpose and a calm approach. Try to perform this meditation twice a day. When you next pass a *real* field of golden sunflowers, you will probably be very tempted to stop and soak in their beauty for a few minutes too!

## Balancing Your Inner and Outer Personality to Improve Your Relationships

Your inborn ability to see the sunnier side of life is a great advantage in relationships because it means that you can help a partner to see things that way too. Because Leo rules the heart you will usually do everything possible within your heart and soul to make a relationship work in the best possible way.

You must not under-estimate the power of love or its importance in your life. A good relationship truly does make the world a better place for you, so it is important to balance your deepest and most sensitive inner emotions with your outer Leo desire for praise and worship by the object of your affections. Sometimes you are a little too inclined to want everything on your terms, without being sufficiently willing to compromise. It's not enough to be romantic and idealistic – you must learn to be a little less fixed in your outer desires and demands. On the surface it could seem wonderful to have someone whom you admire praise you constantly, but if you did not also share a soulmate connection which satisfied the romantic yearnings of your Inner Self, you wouldn't be too happy for long.

Leo is sometimes described as being more interested in the outer trappings of luxury on every level than in spiritual hopes and desires. But if you truly want to create better relationships on your journey through life, remember that they will always be helped along the way by a mind, body and spirit connection on every level.

## A Successful Career

A continuous thread running through the charts of many Leo clients is that you could be considerably more successful than you are. It's not that you don't necessarily make the most of your talents and abilities; more that you sometimes spend far too much time working on projects which won't take you further up the success ladder, and might even have been accepted purely to help out a friend.

If you're a typical Leo you will have masses of creativity

and charm, and deep down I'm sure you will feel that your rightful place is at the top of your profession. But there *is* that slightly lazy side to your Leo personality – sometimes you will slide out of your responsibilities when you can, usually with an excuse that you have been working unbelievably hard until a certain moment when you simply *have* to rest. At other times you may decide that you simply cannot exist without a busy social life, but make sure that you do not neglect important tasks just because you feel like going out and having fun.

It is true that many of you have moments of extreme energy which go hand in hand with a certain lethargic air, but if you do want to be more successful in your career it is important that you learn to balance these a little better. Since at heart you are deeply goal-oriented, never miss a chance to make your mark upon the world. Star quality is inherent within your sign – but it has to be worked upon!

# 7

# Virgo
# 22 August –
# 21 September

VIRGO

If you were born between 22 August and 21 September, you were born under the sixth sign of the Zodiac, the critical and analytical, dedicated and discriminating Virgo. You are a Feminine, Mutable, Negative sign, the second of the Earth signs; your planetary ruler is Mercury, planet of communication, and your planetary symbol is the Virgin. In basic terms, you're one of the real workers of the Zodiac, and astrologers call you 'the sign of service', for you are extremely conscientious and responsible.

If you're a typical Virgo you seem to search for perfection in everything you do, but unfortunately you sometimes worry far too much if you don't find it. In my earlier book, *Carole Golder's Star Signs* (Henry Holt, 1994), is a quote from Oscar Wilde: 'better to take pleasure in a rose than to put its root under a microscope', a maxim which applies to many Virgos. Some of you are incredibly critical of yourselves, when you really have no cause for complaint. You have a great sense of humour, but often it's buried deep within you, only coming to the surface when you've convinced yourself that you have done sufficient work. Try not to be 'the sign of service' every minute of every day! Even a hard-working Virgo is allowed to have some time off to have fun, and it will help to recharge those overworked batteries and allow your inner being to slow down.

Sometimes you are so busy criticising yourself for the faults that probably only *you* perceive that your view of life takes on a somewhat jaundiced position. But once you learn to believe in your own inner strengths, and nurture your positive assets, you won't need to fall back on those self-critical ways because you will believe in yourself and your capabilities a whole lot more. A Virgo client once said that he had heard a colleague describe him as a pessimistic perfectionist, and that it had immediately made him determined to become a great deal more *optimistic* from then on. He succeeded brilliantly, so I'm sure you can do the same

## *Your Ruling Planet*

Your ruling planet is Mercury, and in mythology Mercury was the winged messenger of the Gods, and is the planet of communication. If you're a typical Virgo, this planet's influence will enhance your pragmatic and organisational approach to almost everything in life. It represents your rational mind, and enables you to demonstrate the strength of your mental qualities by lifting you out of your earth-bound self to the heights of your imagination and inspiration.

If you take advantage of Mercury's influence in its most positive sense it will enable you to broaden your vision and view the future with greater optimism and enthusiasm. You will achieve greater clarity of thought and will learn not to worry about the things that might never happen (so often that is one of your major faults)! You will become even more brilliant in your powers of analysis and criticism, because Mercury will enable you to not only understand more about your strengths and weaknesses, but also to communicate more with your Inner Self and to understand your deepest feelings.

Since Mercury was the winged messenger of the Gods, its influence will help you to be more 'mercurial' in your thoughts and actions, letting them flow easier and faster. Mercury also rules the Air sign, Gemini, adding to the mental agility and nervous energy of most Gemini men and women. But in Virgo it enables you to organise your analytical thoughts and enhances your quick comprehension and intellectual prowess, while at the same time keeping your feet firmly on the ground. If you're a typical Virgo you can spot a mistake a mile away, and woe betide an unsuspecting sales person who tries to convince a Virgo customer that a lop-sided hem on an expensive outfit is straight!

Use the power of Mercury to communicate with your higher mind and it will help you to have an even more successful journey through life, achieving your goals along the way. Vow not to analyse why you *cannot* do something from now on — analyse the best way to do it to make it really work!

# *Your Ascendant and Moon Sign*

As discussed in Chapter 1, you will find that you take on something of the personality of the sign that was rising when you were born. If your Ascendant is Virgo, remember that the Mercury influence will be stronger too.

A Virgo with Aries rising will definitely make you more positive and enthusiastic, but don't be too headstrong; a Taurus Ascendant will heighten a desire for your creature comforts to balance all your hard work; a Gemini Ascendant will highlight your communicative skills, but also lighten your analytical and critical views; while Cancer rising will make you more sensitive and emotional than the usual cool Virgo personality. With Leo rising you will have more of a sparkling outer personality, and even enjoy the limelight too; a Virgo Ascendant *could* make you a pessimistic perfectionist, but hopefully a positive one; Libra rising helps to balance your critical ways with a deep desire for peace and harmony; while a Scorpio Ascendant gives an incisive thrust to your analytical views and brings you a brilliant memory. Sagittarius rising means you will be far more outgoing and optimistic, and not quite so keen to find fault; a Capricorn Ascendant will probably make you even more cautious, and especially critical of anyone else's spendthrift ways; Aquarius rising will make you more unconventional and unpredictable than most Virgo men or women; and, finally, your opposite sign of Pisces as your Ascendant could make you somewhat vague but a lot more romantic.

The Moon in your horoscope highlights both your emotions and your innermost needs. It will naturally have an effect on your star sign personality. As a Virgo, with the Moon in Aries you will be far more outgoing and impulsive emotionally; a Taurus Moon enhances your desire for romance and sensuality in your life; a Gemini Moon gives a lighter touch to your serious views on life; and the Moon in Cancer could mean you're a moody nitpicker at bad moments, but a wonderfully caring and realistic human being the rest of the time! A Leo Moon will make you more playful without losing your practical attitude; a Virgo Moon could have you analysing everything that's positive *and* negative about your emotions and innermost needs, hopefully with good results; a Libra Moon will make you appreciate the benefits of lots of tender, loving care; while a Scorpio Moon will enhance your sexuality and make you a more private person too. A Sagittarius Moon will make you emotionally more outgoing and more positive in your innermost beliefs; a Capricorn Moon will highlight your material needs and not just those innermost ones; an Aquarius Moon adds unconventionality to your feelings and an air of detachment too; and, finally, the Moon in Pisces will make you appreciate how wonderful romance can be when you don't keep worrying about it!

## Accentuate the Positive and Reduce the Negative

Remember that 'to err is human' – as long as you learn something from a mistake, and don't repeat it all the time. It is important to tell *you* this because if you're a typical Virgo you are so critical of yourself and of everyone else that you miss out on some of the good aspects of life. Don't be quite so hard on yourself – it's not necessary for you to be a paragon of virtue all the time. Learn to see perfection in what you have, and don't insist on magnifying your faults to yourself and feeding your mind with insecure feelings. It's great to be analytical and discerning, but not if you go over the top instead of looking at the overall picture. Maximise your powers of analysis and discrimination in a constructive way, and they will be a brilliant asset to your Virgo personality.

One way for you to accentuate your positive aspects (which include being exceptionally alert and bright) is to lighten up a little, and vow not to be such a hypochondriac about your health. If you can learn to live more freely and have faith in what lies ahead, you will be able to relax and enjoy your journey through life in a much more positive way.

## Challenges and Obstructions

Sometimes you create unnecessary challenges and conflicts for yourself by being so fussy about everything, whether it is what you do or what everyone else is doing. What makes it worse is that some of you seem to carry an enormous martyr complex upon your shoulders, as though being designated as 'the sign of service' was a cross for you to bear throughout your life, whereas in truth many of you secretly revel in the title.

Everyone has to deal with challenges and obstructions in their life at some point, but there is a tendency within the Virgo personality for you to take them too seriously, even when they are minor. Disciplined and fastidious, dedicated and dutiful, you will deal with problems in a highly organised way. But try not to spend quite so much time on inconsequential details just because you hate to leave any stone unturned. You will be much more successful if you learn to truly understand the inner workings of your Virgo personality, and allow some moments of real rest and relaxation to help recharge your overworked batteries. This is when you will benefit from meditating to help you to become calmer.

## Your Star Sign Meditation to Help You Create a Better Life

☆ Sit comfortably on the floor in a cross-legged position (or, if this is not comfortable, on a chair).

☆ Close your eyes and visualise yourself sitting in one of the most beautiful rooms you have ever seen, with one of your favourite pieces of music playing gently in the background. The décor is simple, the colours pure, and the whole atmosphere is one of calm and tranquillity. Immediately you realise that you have nothing to criticise or be negative about.

☆ Allow your mind to be still and let it simply soak in the beauty; if any thoughts do enter your mind simply let them slip by without worrying about them.

☆ Let yourself sink into this meditative state for approximately 20 minutes, so that you have sufficient time to take the calm and tranquillity deeper into your subconscious mind.

Try to perform this meditation twice a day. You will soon discover that your attitude to life will become more positive, and that when you do feel highly stressed, you can bring the calm back into your mind by simply closing your eyes for a few seconds and imagining that beautiful peaceful room.

Learn to look at the beauty all around you, appreciate it for what it is, and don't try to judge whether it matches up to your own view of perfection. It will be perfect in its own way – which is good enough!

## Balancing Your Inner and Outer Personality to Improve Your Relationships

If you're totally honest, you might want to admit that sometimes you tend to analytically dissect relationships almost to the point of no return.

If you truly want to balance your inner and outer personality, it might help to think of the inner one as a little child who really wants to have fun. Meanwhile, the more disciplined, analytical *outer* you is constantly determined to be the sign of service and the critic of just about everyone and everything – including yourself. Once you can learn to appreciate yourself for all the good things you have within you, you will soon be able to appreciate everyone else a whole lot more too. Stop trying to be the paragon of virtue – you must realise that it's almost impossible for anyone to live with one of those anyway! Balance your own emotional needs with the determination to try to understand a partner's emotional needs better. Affirm to yourself that you will learn to see things more through your heart, and not only with your discriminating mind. And take a tip from romantic Pisces, your opposite sign in the Zodiac – believe in the magic of your dreams so that you can make other people believe in them too.

## A Successful Career

You are usually brilliant at all the practical details involved with your particular work, and are probably one of the most organised people around. You are meticulous in your approach to almost everything, and rarely refuse to put in overtime when necessary, but you could be even more successful, and creatively fulfilled if only you'd learn to overcome insecurity and self-doubt. One Virgo client spent his whole working life worrying about his performance and whether he was appreciated enough, and when he finally retired at a very high level on a very good pension he even spent his time worrying about how to relax and enjoy himself.

Sometimes you let yourself be taken advantage of by colleagues and end up doing their work as well, which is definitely taking the 'sign of service' a bit too far. Do this if you must, but please don't let them take the praise for your efforts, or complain about it afterwards. You are highly competent and capable, and are invariably the sort of person who is completely indispensable in your working environment. But you do have a tendency to sit back and take second place on many of those occasions when you should be climbing higher up the ladder to success.

If you are determined to become more successful in your career, always use your talents in a positive way, and start to blow your trumpet a little more loudly.

# 8

# Libra
# 22 September –
# 22 October

If you were born between 22 September and 22 October, you were born under the seventh sign of the Zodiac, the diplomatic and fair-minded, charming and generous Libra. You are a Masculine, Cardinal, Positive sign, the second of the Air signs; your planetary ruler is Venus, Goddess of Love, and your planetary symbol is the only inanimate object in the Zodiac — the Scales. You have a fantastic ability to help to balance other people's lives with your sense of justice and fair play, but you are not always so good at balancing your own scales, especially when it comes to making decisions.

Your desire for peace and harmony at all costs is noble, but certain Librans carry this much too far, even sometimes backing down from a confrontation when the right is all on their side. Astrologers often call Libra a 'lazy' sign, however many Librans manage to juggle high-flying careers with busy domestic lives, and this 'lazy' aspect is rarely seen. What *is* demonstrated in some Librans is procrastination, which is perhaps your greatest fault.

My mentor, the late, great Patric Walker – himself a Libran – used to say that you always have something to learn about yourself from your opposite sign in the Zodiac. As an Aries, I accept gratefully that the Libran ability to weigh things up before rushing headlong into almost everything in typical Aries mode, is only one of the lessons to be learned. Meanwhile, overly indecisive Librans will also benefit from a little more of the Aries 'go-getter' approach to life! Perhaps it is because your sign commences with the start of autumn, and you stand back as if contemplating what the winter will bring.

One of your greatest lessons is to learn to balance your outer personality with your inner personality, because when you can do this successfully, you will have greater faith in yourself, and find it much easier to make decisions without fearing the consequences of making a wrong judgement.

## *Your Ruling Planet*

One of the reasons you are so in love with beauty, peace and harmony is probably because Venus, Goddess of Love (who is also the ruler of Taurus), is your ruling planet. Venus endows you with a love of colour, light and serenity, and the ability to smile sweetly even when you are hurting deep inside.

But, with Venus as your planetary ruler, you often appear to be in love with love itself. You have an extremely romantic and poetic nature and an idealistic one too! Some of you seem to feel only half complete if you are not part of a couple, and that seems to stand even if you are with someone you feel deep down is wrong for you. Too often you have the tendency to think that a perfect relationship is the only thing worth having in life, and that your Libran scales will remain unbalanced until you find that ideal partner. It's almost as though you deliberately blind yourself to any problems, and forget about your immense need for inner harmony too.

Romantic idealism is all very well, but if you are prepared to analyse yourself, you will agree that you have great inner strength even if you don't feel inclined to show it. This strength will enable you to cushion any disappointments and even to become quite ruthless when you know that someone or something is *really* wrong for you. However, it often takes you a long time to reach your decision and meanwhile you can suffer inwardly.

Venus will highlight your physical desires, and while your passions may be charmingly understated they are most certainly a part of your personality. Just like Taurus, there is even quite a sybaritic side to you, which can make you yearn for beautiful people *and* beautiful objects around you at whatever cost. Venus also gives you great appreciation for harmony in your surroundings, and anything that is cluttered or appears anything less than perfect seems to upset your equilibrium.

It's wonderful to have Venus as your ruling planet and to be able to see the beauty that other signs may often overlook. But don't be so concerned with balancing your partnerships with other people that you overlook the need to be in greater balance with yourself.

## Your Ascendant and Moon Sign

As discussed earlier it is likely that you will take on something of the personality of the sign that was rising when you were born. If your Ascendant is Libra, remember that the Venus influence will be stronger too.

As a Libran with Aries rising you will enjoy putting thoughts and ideas into action, rather than letting them remain as ideals; a Taurus Ascendant heightens your desire for beauty and you'll be much more strong-willed; a Gemini Ascendant enables you to come up with innovative ways to get projects properly off the ground; while a Cancer Ascendant combines Cancer's highly attuned instincts with your logic and rationality. Leo rising will make you more exuberant and fond of the limelight; a Virgo Ascendant will accentuate your ability to analyse but make you even more of a perfectionist; a Libran Ascendant will give you a double dose of charm, tact and diplomacy, but make it more necessary to balance your Libran scales too; and Scorpio rising makes decision-making easier, and heightens your passionate desires. A Sagittarius Ascendant adds greater self-confidence but could make you more extravagant; Capricorn rising will make you work hard to achieve your material objectives, but don't forget your need for balance; an Aquarius Ascendant reduces your need for a partner as you'll feel more inwardly free; and, finally, Pisces rising adds lashings of sensitivity combined with creativity plus an impractical streak.

The Moon in your horoscope highlights both your emotions and your innermost needs. It will naturally have an effect on your star sign personality. As a Libran with the Moon in Aries you will be more impatient in your quest for inner satisfaction; a Taurus Moon brings the double influence of Venus so that you'll be even more romantic; a Gemini Moon will highlight your need to talk things through, but you will perhaps be more fickle; while a Cancer Moon accentuates your emotional needs and might make you somewhat moody at Full Moon times! A Leo Moon possibly makes you even more determined to be in love; a Virgo Moon could make you excessively critical of yourself and everyone else; the Moon in Libra will really inspire you to balance your outer and inner personality as perfectly as you can; while a Scorpio Moon will add heightened intensity to your innermost needs and bring a need for your own private space. A Sagittarius Moon adds to your Libran charm and makes you more free-and-easy in your attitude; a Capricorn Moon highlights your need for security on every level; an Aquarius Moon makes you much less reliant on a partner and more unconventional; and, lastly, a Pisces Moon makes you yearn for lots of tender, loving care.

## Accentuate the Positive and Reduce the Negative

In order to present a more positive face to the world, try making some decisions for yourself, without asking your husband, wife, lover, friend or boss for advice. Once you've discovered that you can manage this perfectly well on your own, it will save you lots of time and trouble in the future.

Resolve to take a tip from your opposite sign of Aries. This doesn't mean that you must suddenly turn into an impulsive and headstrong Ram, but you could try sometimes to be more enthusiastic and energetic even if deep down you feel laid-back and lethargic. You will never lose your sense of fair play. Even if you do hate to become involved in anything that might upset the harmony you need, it is important for you to see that justice is done, even if it means having the courage of your convictions.

'Patience is a virtue' is a maxim that all Ariens should learn, but for Librans perhaps it should be 'procrastination is the root of all evil' – that is, if you want to have an even more successful journey through your life.

## Challenges and Obstructions

Always maximise the potential of your inborn sense of timing and combine it with your logical thought process when you come up against challenges and obstructions. But never bury your head in the sand hoping that they will go away because invariably this will be counter-productive, and is simply an example of Libran procrastination! An interesting challenge will get your energy level flowing and make your mental skills even more agile.

Your ability to see both sides of a given situation will be a great advantage; because it will enable you to judge whether in some way you are perhaps creating certain problems yourself. But sitting on the fence is not the way to get ahead in today's world, nor is being too indecisive in your thoughts and ideas, especially when you *are* faced with any kind of challenge.

Because you hate arguments of any kind, you will try hard not to become involved in them. But this does not mean you should give in on something when you know deep down you are right, for this would be a sign of weakness to the opposing side, and only create more ongoing problems for you.

### YOUR STAR SIGN MEDITATION TO HELP YOU CREATE A BETTER LIFE

☆ Choose a quiet place where no one will disturb you, and sit comfortably on the floor in a cross-legged position (or, if this is not comfortable, on a chair).

☆ Close your eyes and visualise two beautiful golden balls floating in the air above you. As you watch them, you will see that first one ball is continually higher than the other, and then the second one keeps taking the higher position.

☆ Allow your mind to be still, but don't worry if thoughts keep coming in; let them drift by and visualise the two balls reaching a perfect balance so that they are level with each other.

☆ Let yourself sink into a meditative state for approximately 20 minutes, and if one of the golden balls goes higher than its partner, just visualise it balancing out again.

☆ Let them be perfectly balanced before you open your eyes once more.

Try to perform this meditation twice a day and you will soon find that your Libran personality will become more balanced, enabling you to become more decisive and successful in your journey through life.

And any time you do find yourself becoming confused or uncertain about an important decision, just close your eyes for a moment and think of those two beautifully balanced golden balls – it really will help.

## Balancing Your Inner and Outer Personality to Improve Your Relationships

Relating well to other people is often one of your finest assets – especially as Libra rules the seventh house, which is the house of partnerships. Many Librans feel that they are simply not complete if they are not in a relationship, however if they learn to feel complete within themselves, they will find it much easier to attract a good relationship. In your desire to please, many of you sometimes attract the wrong people to your side. You love to be in the company of others, and are often too kind and generous to people who take advantage of this. There is also a somewhat self-indulgent side to your Libran personality, and a certain immaturity within relationships. Too often you are moved by what you *think* is right for you, without necessarily feeling this deeply.

If you're a typical Libran, the idea of finding an everlasting soulmate is very inviting. But when you open yourself up to your inner voice, you will discover that your deepest needs also relate to being in tune with yourself, and not simply to be in tune with someone else's needs. You will learn to balance your yearning for romance with greater inner strength and with the knowledge that you can manage perfectly well on your own when necessary. This in turn will help stop you involving yourself ever again in those relationships whose only real benefit is to prevent you from spending time alone with *you*.

## A Successful Career

There is a certain complaisance within your Libran personality which makes you sit back and wait for the work to come to you, rather than going out and searching for the chance to become more of a success. Unfortunately, in today's fast-paced work environment this will sometimes mean that you lose out on good opportunities. It is always important to maximise the potential of your inborn sense of timing, your logical thought processes, and your ability to communicate your thoughts effectively to a wide variety of people. You cannot afford to be too laid-back and nonchalant in your actions if you want to get ahead in your chosen career.

When you *do* commit yourself to any plans or projects you become a master of strategy, but often it's the vacillation or indecision that takes place first that leaves you in second place. You must be able to prove that you can be an entrepreneurial achiever with shrewd negotiating skills (although this definitely doesn't mean that you have to lose your admirable sense of fair play!) and that you have the ability to make quick decisions when they are necessary.

If you are determined to become more successful in your career, always remember to balance your Libran scales on every level. Look at yourself inwardly and make sure you recognise your talents *and* any limitations. But resolve that you will never hold yourself back by doubting yourself unnecessarily, because you are blessed with the ability to fulfil your ambitions.

# 9

# Scorpio
# 23 October –
# 21 November

If you were born between 23 October and 21 November, you were born under the eighth sign of the Zodiac, the magnetic and charismatic, intense and highly emotional Scorpio. You are a Feminine, Fixed, Negative sign, the second of the Water signs. Both Mars, the God of War, and Pluto, the Lord of the Underworld, are your planetary rulers; your planetary symbol is the Scorpion, but both the Serpent and the Eagle are linked symbolically with your sign. In basic terms, you tend to be invincible when it comes to achieving your goals, but many of you have a self-destructive side to your personality.

Scorpio is renowned as the 'sex symbol of the Zodiac' and often you will take every opportunity to demonstrate the truth of this description. But underneath that seemingly tough exterior often beats the heart of a highly vulnerable human being. You feel everything so strongly that unless you're truly at peace with yourself deep within it is often hard for you to be happy with yourself. You take life immensely seriously and your sense of authority seems to come from almost mystical depths of hidden power. There is also a very private side to your personality that you almost seem to hide away from yourself. Possessive and jealous, you guard your own privacy zealously, and woe betide anyone who tries to get too close to your Scorpio secrets.

If you're a typical Scorpio you are a sign of great extremes, with moments of deep suffering alternating with those of deep joy at achieving a certain objective. Sometimes you may feel that you are a loner who is forced into a desperate search to fulfil your deepest emotions. But if you learn to communicate more with your inner being you will find it easier to achieve greater peace and happiness in your journey through life.

Creating the perfect balance between your inner and outer personality is not always easy, but as an invincible Scorpio you can rise to the challenge! It is important for you to see the positive side of life, and not to take everything quite so seriously. Scorpio is one of the most maligned signs of the Zodiac, because people always seem to talk about the dark side of your nature and overlook the fact that you are extremely loyal and caring towards the people in your life.

## Your Ruling Planet

With Mars, the God of War, *and* Pluto, God of the Underworld (whose astrological associations are with the regenerative and creative force of the body), it's hardly surprising that you possess such great inner strength and regenerative powers. But it is important for you to get the right balance of these, and that is why learning to be more in touch with your Inner Self is so necessary.

Mars helps you to fight for everything that you believe in, and to deal with seemingly impossible challenges with enormous energy and great strength. It will also accentuate your passion and sexual drive. Mars is also the planetary ruler of Aries, but *your* Martian power will be more controlled and less impulsive than Aries. However, you must be careful not to allow the negative side of Mars to make you too ruthless or manipulative in your objectives. And make sure you don't become obsessive about your inner fears or insecurities by allowing them to build up inside you.

Pluto will help you to bring things to the surface, and its power will enable you to see beyond the here and now, and to rise above problems which would seem insurmountable to the rest of us. Pluto's influence is responsible not only for your regenerative powers but also for your interest in searching out the deeper mysteries of life.

Pluto also relates to enforced change and to the beginnings and endings of life phases. It is perhaps no surprise that so many people born under the sign of Scorpio are interested in the occult, religion and reincarnation. Scorpio is also the sign of the healer, once you have learned to balance your inner and outer personality, and to expand your vision so that you overcome those dark feelings which perhaps have held you back in the past.

It is wonderful to have both Mars and Pluto as your planetary rulers, for you will always be able to fall back on the enormous reserves of inner strength which they have bequeathed upon you and which are an integral part of your

Scorpio personality. But make sure you use this strength to see the joys that life has to offer, and listen to your inner voice more often if you want to advance spiritually.

## Your Ascendant and Moon Sign

As discussed in Chapter 1, you will take on something of the personality of the sign that was rising when you were born. If your Ascendant is Scorpio, remember that those Mars and Pluto influences will be stronger too.

As a Scorpio with Aries rising you are a fearless and energetic individual – but don't overdo the power complex bit; a Taurus Ascendant will combine your determination to succeed with a more patient approach; Gemini rising will add to your creative skills and give you an altogether lighter view of life; while with Cancer rising you will be much more compassionate and sensitive when you are in your power playing mode. A Leo Ascendant will brighten up your brooding intensity and bring out the lovable part of you; Virgo rising will combine your Scorpio sixth sense with a brilliantly analytical approach to any problems that may come along; a Libra Ascendant will bring charm, tact and diplomacy to that intense and sometimes introverted Scorpio personality; and a Scorpio Ascendant means you're *truly* invincible, but make sure that you are never too cold and calculating on your way to the top! Sagittarius rising makes you much more outgoing, enthusiastic and optimistic about life; a Capricorn Ascendant combines a great sense of duty with your powerful Scorpio insight; an Aquarius Ascendant makes you fixed in your opinions and your feelings – but watch out that you're not too unpredictable; and, finally, a Pisces Ascendant brings more sensitivity and tolerance to a sometimes ruthless Scorpio.

The Moon in your horoscope highlights both your

emotions and your innermost needs. It will naturally have an effect on your star sign personality. As a Scorpio, with the Moon in Aries there will be added fire to your emotions, but an almost childlike innocence too; a Taurus Moon will bring an earthy sensuality and a double dose of determination to fill your innermost needs; a Gemini Moon will make your emotions and needs seem less focused and you'll be more light-hearted; while a Cancer Moon heightens your sensitivity but could make you more vulnerable emotionally. A Leo Moon accentuates a need to be the star of the show, but makes you immensely lovable; a Virgo Moon could make it harder for you to reveal your deepest feelings, even to yourself, and you might be very self-critical; a Libra Moon makes you gentler on other people and also on yourself; while the Moon in Scorpio makes you doubly intense and emotional, but doubly psychic at the same time. A Sagittarius Moon lessens your burning intensity and gives you a much more free-and-easy attitude to everything; a Capricorn Moon brings a down-to-earth attitude to your innermost needs; an Aquarius Moon makes you more unconventional and more detached emotionally; and, lastly, a Pisces Moon softens that brooding Scorpio intensity and makes you tenderly romantic.

## Accentuate the Positive and Reduce the Negative

Because you are extremely psychic, you often know what other people are thinking before they say a word and, deep down, you also know exactly what you need in order to live a satisfying and fulfilled life. One lesson you often need to learn is to overcome that self-destructive side to your personality, that part of you that makes you frustrated, jealous or resentful of other people who seem to be more successful than you. This destructive urge is one of the negative directions that your powerfully creative energy will take if you allow it – all the more reason to learn to balance your inner and outer personalities so that your positive qualities vibrate at the highest level.

When you are truly positive, and use your powerful Scorpio instincts to help you on your journey through life, you will rise above any feelings of insecurity like the proverbial phoenix from the ashes. When you know what you want from life you will usually go after it fearlessly. However, this may lead to recklessness. Do you know that the Scorpion will even sting himself to death when surrounded by a ring of fire? You might not go to those lengths, but it would not do you any harm to become a little more flexible and not quite so intense!

## Challenges and Obstructions

Although many Scorpios possess that famed invincible streak which enables them to deal with major challenges and obstructions in the best possible way, it is often the emotional issues which seem to faze them.

Because you are an extremely private person, it is sometimes hard for you to admit to anyone that you are facing problems. But in many instances that old maxim 'a problem shared is a problem halved' can be extremely worthwhile. If you air your thoughts and feelings to someone that you can trust, you will often discover that your own insight combined with their input will be a big help. Don't be so fixed in your opinions and so adamant that you do not need any outside help that you magnify any challenges and obstructions that you encounter.

If you're a typical Scorpio your burning intensity to get to the root of a problem sometimes leaves you feeling over-stressed. A perfect way to overcome this is to find a meditation which will not only help you to become more calm, but will also enable you to feel more in tune with your Inner Self.

## YOUR STAR SIGN MEDITATION TO HELP YOU CREATE A BETTER LIFE

☆ Sit comfortably on the floor, in a cross-legged position (or, if this is not comfortable, on a chair).

☆ Close your eyes and make sure you are sitting very straight and still.

☆ Let your mind also be still, but don't worry if thoughts come in. Let them float on by, for all that matters is that you imagine you can feel the river of life in your spine.

☆ Feel this river flowing slowly up your spine until it finally reaches the point between your eyebrows. Then imagine that this river, full of energy and light, is bursting forth into a great sea full of cosmic light.

☆ Let yourself bask in this light for approximately 20 minutes, at the end of which time visualise the river continuing slowly along its path, with the cosmic light now just a glow, but with its power ever present.

Try to perform this meditation twice a day. You will soon start to feel more in touch with your mind, body and soul and be able to use your inner power for the highest good, thus creating the necessary balance in your life. And any time you do feel in need of a burst of extra energy, just close your eyes for a moment and think of the river of life and the help it can give you.

## Balancing Your Inner and Outer Personality to Improve Your Relationships

Your feelings are smouldering, intense and passionate, but try to make sure that they do not become so overpowering that you scare off someone you care for in the early stages of a relationship.

The art of sexual seduction is rarely difficult for a typical Scorpio, but in order to create better relationships in your life, it is important to be completely honest about your innermost needs. Many single Scorpio men and women secretly yearn for a true soulmate with whom to share their lives, and a relationship that is based solely on sexual attraction will never last for long.

Sometimes you are accused of being cruel and unfeeling within a relationship, but perhaps that is also because you find it difficult to forgive anyone, let alone forget anything which you think is unfair. Once you learn to balance your inner and outer personality you will also learn to harness your possessive and jealous ways a little more, or resolve not to over-react the next time someone behaves possessively towards you.

You are not always easy to understand, because you can be intense at one moment and totally remote the next. Try to stop taking things to such extremes and avoid battling with your own emotions. Start to open yourself up more and trust in your intuition. Recognise the need within you for a partner whom you can respect for their own inner strength, because someone who is weak will only bring out negative qualities in you.

Remember that when you have achieved the balance within yourself it will become a whole lot easier to achieve it with every other sign.

## A Successful Career

If you're a typical Scorpio, you will invariably strive courageously to reach the top in your chosen career, and your self-driven warrior spirit will always sustain you in your determination to become more successful. You have a shrewd mind, a phenomenal memory and almost uncanny intuition. You enjoy competing for a chosen goal, but must never let a determination to win, or an inherent desire for power and control, to alienate the very people you need to have on your side.

If you truly want to be more successful you must never block your creative talents and abilities by giving way to hidden insecurities or by becoming ruthless or manipulative in your working methods. You have tremendous drive and above-average powers of concentration, so always make sure that you work in a field that truly stretches your mind. And always focus on the long-term consequences of your actions and not simply on the short-term ones.

Your self-driven warrior spirit will always sustain you in your determination to become more successful, as will your burning desire for greater knowledge of life itself. But watch out that you don't burn up your Martian energy and end up feeling angry or stressed-out if things become tough in today's fast-moving workplace. Remember that you will always benefit from the regenerative powers of Pluto (your other ruling planet). Believe in yourself at a deep soul level and you will always find ways to be successful in your chosen career.

# 10

# Sagittarius
# 22 November –
# 20 December

If you were born between 22 November and 20 December, you were born under the ninth sign of the Zodiac, the optimistic and outgoing, free-spirited and free-thinking Sagittarius. You are a Masculine, Mutable, Positive sign, and the last of the Fire signs; your planetary ruler is Jupiter, planet of good fortune, and the Centaur with his arrow is your planetary symbol. In simple terms, you're one of the most adventurous and resilient signs of the Zodiac, with a good sense of humour and a bright and sunny disposition.

If you're a typical Sagittarius, one particular aspect of your personality shows that you are almost incapable of being dishonest, although that can sometimes be a disadvantage. You can be extremely tactless at the wrong moment, perhaps not even realising what you have said until you notice the mortified look on the face of your listener. Honesty is one thing, but giving unwanted opinions is not always the best way to win friends and influence people. I know it must be wonderful to be described astrologically as 'the sign of the higher mind' and the 'sage and counsellor of the Zodiac', but often a little more diplomacy will be beneficial too. Don't insist on moralising to everyone else and always make sure you are considerate of other people's points of view.

You are definitely a survivor and your amazingly positive attitude to life enables you to rise above setbacks which would send the rest of us reeling and might take us months to get over. Never lose your wonderful belief in life and all the good things it has to offer you for it truly is one of your most positive characteristics. You have a strong sense of survival that will always enable you to rise above even the darkest moments.

## Your Ruling Planet

You are fortunate to have Jupiter as your planetary ruler, because in mythology Jupiter was the great benefactor who represented growth and expansion on the earth; and Jupiter will be beneficial to you – provided you use its power wisely.

Astrologically, Jupiter is known as the planet of good fortune. Jupiter may indeed bring you luck, but you must be prepared to make the most of good opportunities when they come your way. Jupiter influences your desire for higher knowledge, and your interest in learning more about the deeper meaning of life. This planetary ruler highlights your optimism and self-confidence, and accentuates your spirit of adventure. Jupiter is also conscience in its deepest sense and it brings you your inner sense of law and order. But never take Jupiter's influence for granted, for it can also make you careless, optimistic and extravagant in your thoughts and actions, to the extent that you seem to expect success without giving anything in return! It is important to learn to integrate your inner and outer personality and to find your own true path in life, for if not, the influence of Jupiter can lead you to become too much of a dilettante, trusting too much to fortunate opportunities that might come your way.

One of the many benefits of learning more about astrology in general, and especially about how to bring out the more positive aspects of your sign, is that you will enjoy finding out more about your ruling planet, and how to make the best possible use of its beneficial attributes. In mythology, the Romans considered Jupiter to be the protector of justice and virtue, and with his qualities of wisdom and optimism he was the most powerful of all the Gods. Interestingly enough, in Sanskrit, Jupiter was known as Guru, 'the spiritual teacher or guide', teaching us about the principles of life.

It is wonderful to have Jupiter as your planetary ruler, for it will enable you to expand your consciousness on every level, and to broaden your horizons both mentally and physically. It will also enable you to live life to the full, courageously and expansively, and will provide you with that winning streak which seems to be inherent within your Sagittarius personality!

## Your Ascendant and Moon Sign

As discussed in Chapter 1, in principle, you will take on something of the personality of the sign that was rising when you were born. If your Ascendant is Sagittarius, remember that the Jupiter influence will be stronger too.

A Sagittarius with Aries rising will make you even more enthusiastic and enterprising, but take care you're not *too* fiery and impulsive; Taurus rising will add practicality to your optimism, and realism to your adventurous spirit; Gemini rising will mean you could be very restless, so you'll need to become self-disciplined in your ways; and a Cancer Ascendant makes you more domesticated and security conscious than many other free-spirited Sagittarians. Leo rising could make you excessively flamboyant and extravagant, so do take great care; a Virgo Ascendant will tone down any careless attributes and make you work hard to achieve your objectives; Libra rising will give you tact, diplomacy and the ability to see both sides of an argument before making your point; while a Scorpio Ascendant will make you intensely determined to succeed in everything you undertake and give you lots of added sex appeal too. A Sagittarius Ascendant means you'll be the life and soul of every party, but perhaps just *too* lackadaisical in your approach to life; Capricorn rising will tone down your happy-go-lucky approach by adding maturity and realism to your personality; an Aquarius Ascendant will make you a searcher for the truth, and a true believer in worthy ideas; and, finally, Pisces rising will make you more sensitive, intuitive and compassionate – and more of a romantic idealist!

The Moon in your horoscope highlights both your emotions and your innermost needs. It will naturally have an effect on your star sign personality. As a Sagittarius, with the Moon in Aries, you will be a happy-go-lucky soul with an optimistic approach emotionally; a Taurus Moon will give you a more serious approach to life; a Gemini Moon makes you an entertaining social butterfly; and a Cancer Moon means your adventurous spirit has an inner need for emotional security. A Leo Moon heightens your extrovert ways and also your need to feel loved; a Virgo Moon could make you feel determined to analyse your innermost needs and your emotional ones too; a Libra Moon will make you far more open-minded about what you're searching for deep down, and more romantic at the same time; while a Scorpio Moon makes you far more possessive and jealous than most Sagittarians, and much more intense about everything too. A Sagittarius Moon accentuates just about every trait you already possess on the surface and will put them at soul level; a Capricorn Moon makes your adventurous spirit yearn for more security on almost every level; the Moon in Aquarius makes you a genuine individualist but it could be hard to know exactly what you *do* need deep inside; and, finally, a Pisces Moon adds a fascinating blend of romanticism to your expansive spirit and socialising ways.

## Accentuate the Positive and Reduce the Negative

It might be hard to imagine that you could be *more* positive than you already are, for you are definitely one of the most positive signs in the Zodiac, with masses of optimism, an adventurous disposition plus your great sense of humour. If you're a typical Sagittarius, you have plenty of self-confidence and self-assurance, and once you harness your tendency to go over the top in some of your words and actions you will be able to have a successful and smooth journey through life.

Having told you just how positive you are, it seems almost unfair to mention negativity. But there are often occasions when you moralise a little too much to the rest of us, and you do have a habit of always thinking that you know best — even when sometimes you don't. You may also be prone to exaggeration, extravagance, extremism and excessive em-bellishment of the truth! You also don't really like to be given advice by anyone else, preferring to follow your own. And, brilliant as you are at coming up with amazing ideas to help you conquer the world, you are not always quite as brilliant at coping with the nitty-gritty involved in putting those same ideas into action. Listen to your inner voice more often — but take its advice too!

## Challenges and Obstructions

You have an amazing ability to rise above disappointments, and always manage to be humorous about them. But, equally, you can be almost too nonchalant about the challenges or obstructions you encounter, or appear to rely a little too much on Jupiter's 'good fortune'.

Sometimes you have too many things going on in your restless mind at once, so that it then becomes difficult for you to think about any one of them in a clearheaded way. You must be more organised and analytical in order to deal with problems because otherwise you will make a wrong decision far too easily.

In many ways, your optimistic personality thrives on challenges, but you like to be able to resolve difficulties without much trouble, and are far too inclined to take the easy way out and simply assume that you will be able to achieve good results. Learn to be as good at listening to constructive advice as you are at telling other people what is best for *them*! And be open to the benefits of meditation to make you become calm and in tune with your own inner voice too.

## Your Star Sign Meditation to Help You Create a Better Life

☆ Sit comfortably on the floor in a cross-legged position (or, if this is not comfortable, on a chair).

☆ Close your eyes and visualise a beautiful purple velvet cloth spread out in front of you with an arrow lying upon it.

☆ Visualise this arrow (the symbol of Sagittarius) shooting up towards the stars, and tune into its vibrations of love, peace and joy.

☆ Allow your mind to be still, but don't worry if thoughts do insist on coming in. Think of them as stars that will shower you with greater spiritual awareness and a sense of higher consciousness, and let them pass on by.

☆ Let yourself sink slowly into a meditative state for approximately 20 minutes, so that you have the time to visualise the stars glowing in the sky, and allow their spiritual gifts to enter your sub-conscious mind.

Try to perform this meditation twice a day. You will soon start to feel the benefit in your daily life and will find it easier to channel your boundless energy, enthusiasm and your philosophy of life in even more positive ways. When you next look up at the night sky, watching the stars will become even more pleasurable too, knowing they contain their own special message for you.

## Balancing Your Inner and Outer Personality to Improve Your Relationships

On the surface you appear to be self-confident, sparkling, and free as a bird, without the slightest problem in achieving really good relationships. But many Sagittarians often find it hard to balance their outwardly freedom-loving ways with an inner need for emotional security.

If you're a typical Sagittarius, you value your freedom perhaps more than any other Zodiac sign. Freedom of speech and freedom of action are a part of your make-up. But it may be that you don't appreciate the fact that it is perfectly possible to feel *inwardly* free and still enjoy a successful and permanent relationship. Of course, this will also depend on your partner, so that if you choose to be involved with someone who is possessive and jealous of your every move it will become very difficult.

Be idealistic about romance, but be realistic too. Don't go full steam ahead without being honest about your innermost feelings. If you truly want to create better relationships, it is extremely important that you know, deep down at soul level, what you need in order to make you feel happy and contented. But remember that if you refuse to change anything about your freedom-at-all-costs personality it will be more difficult to have a successful one-on-one relationship. Meanwhile, at least you can try to control some of your restless ways, and learn to define your relationship goals a little more clearly – both inwardly *and* outwardly.

## A Successful Career

Although you are sometimes wildly optimistic, and overly ambitious with grandiose expectations of what life has to offer you, many Sagittarians have a very high success rate in their careers, often in more than one career too. Your boundless enthusiasm combined with your belief in yourself and your abilities is a lot more positive than under-valuing yourself. Jupiter's influence enables you to see good career possibilities where others may see only difficulties.

You are able to operate on your own initiative with flair and entrepreneurial ability. But in order to be more successful, or hold on to the success you have already achieved, it is important to recognise that sometimes you do need a more disciplined approach to your working life. Structure and organisation are rarely amongst your favourite words, and you tend to feel stifled if you have to put up with too much routine. However, that is no excuse for scattering your energies too far and wide, or making extravagant promises to your boss or colleagues that you may not be able to keep.

You are not always the most practical person where finances are concerned, so always try to make sure that you are paid fairly in your chosen career. Working on a commission basis might not be the best idea for an overly optimistic Sagittarius, as you could find yourself losing out.

When *you* believe in yourself and your talents, you have the inherent ability to make the rest of the world believe in you too, and with a little more self-discipline you can become even more successful – it's all up to you!

# 11

# Capricorn
# 21 December –
# 19 January

If you were born between 21 December and 19 January, you
were born under the tenth sign of the Zodiac, the ambitious
and disciplined, serious and strong-willed Capricorn. You are
a Feminine, Cardinal, Negative sign, the last of the Earth
signs; your planetary ruler is Saturn, known astrologically as
'Old Father Time', and your planetary symbol is either the
Goat with the curling fish's tail, or as is more usually por-
trayed, the Mountain Goat. In basic terms, you are a dedicated perfectionist and quite a traditionalist too. You are like

the mountain goat that picks its way carefully up a steep and craggy mountain, determined to reach its peak, because your sense of duty and reliable sense of timing enable you to achieve your objectives, no matter how many obstacles you face along the way.

But do you ever inwardly feel you must have been singled out to be one of the real workers of the world? Would you sometimes like to have more fun? The problem with being a typical Capricorn is that even if you *do* think of shirking, your inner soul will not allow it! I often joke about a Capricorn worker being always the last one to leave the office, and maybe there is some truth in this!

If you are typical of your sign, your determination to be successful probably entered the world along with your very first breath. The phrase 'an old head on young shoulders' could have been invented especially for Capricorn children, who seem to view life as a serious business from the start. It is highly admirable to be so self-disciplined and hard working, but never become so concerned with the material side of life that you lose out on your personal happiness. Even a hard-working Capricorn is entitled to some leisure moments, and the chance to relax.

One of my earlier books, *Success Through The Stars* (Henry Holt, 1996), included some advice from a Capricorn, Paramhansa Yogananda: 'Inner harmony is a prolific source of power; it breeds strength'. While it is certainly true that you possess an abundance of strength, you are sometimes lacking in the 'inner harmony' stakes, and tend to worry if you feel you are not achieving sufficient success. Once you learn to balance your inner and outer strengths a little better, you will find you begin to view the world in a much more positive and less pessimistic light.

## *Your Ruling Planet*

One of the major influences on your Capricorn personality is your ruling planet Saturn. In mythology, Saturn (or Chronus) was the oldest of the gods, and in addition to being the keeper of time he was also the lawgiver and taskmaster of everyone on earth. Astrologers tend to call Saturn 'the taskmaster of the Zodiac' but while Saturn may teach us about demands and limitations, his influence will always bring the greatest rewards in the end.

Saturn's influence on you will be of even greater benefit if you learn to balance your inner and your outer life harmoniously, and to combine your stern self-discipline with greater faith in yourself. Saturn takes between 28 and 30 years to go around the Zodiac, and when it returns to the place it occupied at your birth it invariably coincides with a significant period in your life, perhaps even a crisis point, and it teaches you an important lesson. This first period of your life can be difficult, but after that time you will reap the rewards of Saturn's discipline, and be thankful for its influence.

It is immensely interesting to see the two sides of the Capricorn personality – the one which can abuse power and ambition like Richard Nixon, Joseph Stalin and Idi Amin, and the one which leads you into greater spirituality, like Yogananda, Maharishi Mahesh Yogi and Gurdjieff. It's as though you are rarely prepared to do things by half-measures, no matter how rocky the path may be. It is always important for you to balance your inner and outer life so that the material issues don't take precedence over everything else.

One of the most positive effects of having Saturn as your ruling planet is that it represents the structure, order and stability in your life. It also teaches you a great deal about self-preservation and duty, not just to others but also to yourself. Saturn is a powerful influence in your life, and it will help you to become not only more successful, but wiser and more knowledgeable too. It's often known as the planet of limitation and delays — but be happy that its influence will also prevent you from making impulsive moves or rushing in where angels fear to tread.

## Your Ascendant and Moon Sign

You will almost certainly take on something of the personality of the sign that was rising when you were born. If your Ascendant is Capricorn, remember that the Saturn influence will be stronger too.

As a Capricorn with Aries rising you will combine fiery energy with a much more grounded approach to everything; a Taurus Ascendant will accentuate your good timing, sense of responsibility and determination to succeed; a Gemini Ascendant will give you a more light-hearted view of life, with lots of original ideas; while a Cancer Ascendant will help to soften your more sombre Capricorn personality, making you more sensitive. Leo rising will make you more inclined to enjoy a sparkling social life as well as working hard; a Virgo Ascendant will make you one of the most dedicated workaholics in the whole Zodiac; a Libra Ascendant will enable you to balance the pros and cons before making important decisions; while with a Scorpio Ascendant you could have a real power complex, and need to watch the tendency to control or manipulate too much. Sagittarius rising will give you a generally more optimistic view of life, and enable you to be open to new ideas; with Capricorn rising you will never shirk any responsibilities, but really must learn to relax a little more; Aquarius rising will give you a freedom-loving approach to just about everything; and, finally, a Pisces Ascendant will make you more romantic, sentimental and intuitive.

The Moon in your horoscope highlights both your emotions and your innermost needs. It will naturally have an effect on your star sign personality. As a Capricorn, with the Moon in Aries you will be an interesting blend of impulsiveness and holding back; with a Taurus Moon you will be seeking material security in your life but will be exceedingly pragmatic too; a Gemini Moon will make you a much more extrovert personality whose restless ways almost belie your Sun sign; while a Cancer Moon will accentuate a deep inner need for emotional security and traditional values. A Leo Moon will highlight your romantic desires, but could make you extremely dogmatic; the Moon in Virgo doubles your Earth element and makes you even more practical, responsible and serious about everything; a Libra Moon will soften your personality and make you more of a tender, loving, caring person; while the Moon in Scorpio emphasises a really private side in your personality, and sometimes makes it harder to reveal your innermost feelings. The Moon in Sagittarius will always help to make you more optimistic in the romance stakes, and happy-go-lucky in your attitude too; a Capricorn Moon will make you seem even more controlled and disciplined in your feelings and emotions, so don't forget they *do* exist; an Aquarius Moon makes you materialistic in some ways and yet amazingly unpredictable in others; and, lastly, a Pisces Moon will heighten your innermost emotions, idealism and romantic feelings in every possible way.

## Accentuate the Positive and Reduce the Negative

Everything you do seems to be planned extremely carefully, which in itself sounds like positive trait. The trouble is that although your sense of duty is a great attribute, it always makes you appear somewhat of a martyr. It's almost as though you use the influence of Saturn rather like that of a supervisor who gets you to clock in at a certain time, and refuses to allow you to clock out a minute too early.

If you're a typical Capricorn, you tend to feel insecure when you're not in control, or worry incessantly about whether you will have enough in the bank to live on when you're old, even though you *always* tend to have something stashed away for emergencies. But you also have a great sense of humour, so why on earth don't you let it start to show through more often, and resolve to learn to laugh at yourself once in a while too!

Capricorns almost seem to think it a sin if you take a holiday or even a day off from your work. Haven't you ever heard about 'recharging your batteries'? It's crazy to think you can just keep on going without allowing yourself some enjoyable moments of rest and relaxation. Don't be so pessimistic about life, or quite so concerned with your material aims and ambitions. You know that you have an excellent chance of achieving them anyway! Take a leaf out of Sagittarius's book (the sign which precedes yours) and vow that you will start to take a much more positive view of life and even try to be a little more frivolous too.

## Challenges and Obstructions

Always try to deal with any challenges and obstructions in a positive way. You are often much too inclined to take a negative view, which is unnecessary because, just like that mountain goat, you inwardly know that you will invariably arrive at the top of your own mountain.

If you're a typical Capricorn you have an amazing ability to overcome obstacles, and a willingness to learn from any mistakes. But although you usually want to be in control it is always a good idea to listen to the advice of people whose expertise and trust can be relied upon implicitly. If challenges and obstructions do come along, don't simply think that you can do *everything* alone!

There is no need to suggest that you organise yourself better on a work level, but by learning to organise yourself better on a mind, body and soul level you will find it much easier to adapt to any difficult circumstances. You will have greater faith in yourself and your abilities too, especially if you find a meditation that will help you to reach your inner voice.

## YOUR STAR SIGN MEDITATION TO HELP YOU CREATE A BETTER LIFE

☆ Sit comfortably on the floor in a cross-legged position (or, if this is not comfortable, on a chair).

☆ Close your eyes and visualise yourself sitting on a hillside, with your back against a tree.

☆ Keep your spine straight and visualise a flow of spiritual energy passing up through your body towards its seat of concentration which is located at a point midway between your two eyebrows.

☆ Allow your mind to be still, but don't worry if thoughts and ideas insist on coming in – just let them drift on by as if they were clouds above the hillside.

☆ Let yourself sink slowly into a meditative state for approximately 20 minutes, so that you allow the flow of spiritual energy to enter your body and to fill you with positive strength on a mind, body and spirit level.

Try to perform this meditation twice a day. You will soon learn instinctively when your 20 minutes are up. You will discover that you are able to balance your life more so that you find more time for relaxation and learn to stop being quite so hard upon yourself. And next time you feel like recharging those hardworking Capricorn batteries, and the weather is warm, take advantage of a few moments sitting on the ground with your back against a *real* tree, rather than just visualising it, for this can also help.

## Balancing Your Inner and Outer Personality to Improve Your Relationships

Many Capricorns are such workaholics that they find it extremely difficult to sustain a relationship – let alone create a better one! If you're a typical Capricorn you often need to admit deep down that you do *have* emotional needs. Sometimes your outer personality seems to be so remarkably self-contained that is difficult to imagine that you might have a vulnerable side within.

Saturn's influence always gives you a strong sense of duty and responsibility, but there are times when you should per-haps feel duty-bound to get more in touch with the Inner You. When you delve deeper into your Inner Self, you will learn to be less structured in your rigid routines and also learn to love yourself for who you are and not for what you can achieve. Once you have started to do this you will be able to create better relationships too.

Are you one of those real Capricorn workaholics who wishes that you could fulfil your romantic needs a little more easily? Do you secretly dream of creating the perfect relationship – yet fear the thought of showing your vulnerability? If any of this applies to you, try to believe in the magic of your dreams for once – it really can work!

## A Successful Career

The way you achieve your goals is often admirable – even if you start at the bottom you will use your self-discipline, persistence and determination to get ahead and reach the top, no matter how long it might take you. But sometimes you become so carried away with your aims and objectives that you start to demonstrate a ruthless streak which alienates people, especially those whose co-operation you might need.

Although you possess the ability to turn mere concepts into successful realities, you can also be too much of a perfectionist and much too hard on yourself. It's wonderful to have high standards, but try not to make a colleague's life a misery just because he (or she) is not as intrinsically ambitious as you are. You seem to have your feet firmly on the ground, and will rarely take the slightest risk, but sometimes you need to be a little more open to new ways of doing things. If you learn to be conversant with all the latest technology it could even mean you don't have to be the last one to leave the office – but then what would you do!

It's always important for you to balance your material ambitions with the way you want to feel deep inside. You will invariably possess the inherent ability to climb to the top of your chosen mountain peak, but never lose sign of your inner values along the way.

# 12

# Aquarius
# 20 January –
# 18 February

If you were born between 20 January and 18 February, you were born under the eleventh sign of the Zodiac, the unconventional and unpredictable, idealistic and independent Aquarius. You are a Masculine, Fixed, Positive sign, and the last of the Air signs; your planetary ruler is Uranus, planet of invention (although before Uranus was discovered in 1781 Saturn was associated with your sign), and your planetary symbol is the Water Bearer. In basic terms, you're the truth seeker and humanitarian of the Zodiac, an idealist with a social conscience, determined to leave your mark upon the world – the original rebel with (or without) a cause!

There doesn't seem to be a stereotypical Aquarian, and I often describe you as the sort of person who behaves wonderfully when you fear the worst, or the contrary when everyone expects everything to be sweetness and light! It is hard to find common characteristics in Aquarians – you are all unique and that is what you were born to be. You are original in thought and independent in manner, and you have a great deal to offer. But sometimes you insist on taking too firm a stand on the issues you believe in. You should be more prepared to see both sides of a situation, and to take a more balanced approach to life.

Sometimes you can be extremely irritating, because just when other people think they are beginning to understand your personality, you will become very stubborn and rigid in your outlook. Wanting to make the world into a better place always sounds wonderful in theory, but you often land yourself in unnecessary trouble because of your words and actions. If you want to have an easier journey through life, it will help if you take that 'truth seeker' description of Aquarius, and learn to understand the truth about *yourself*, at deep soul level. By doing this you will also learn to balance your Aquarian traits of inspiration and idealism with reality and practicality, and become more tolerant of those signs who simply don't want to be as unconventional as you. You will also find the right balance between your sense of duty to the world and your sense of duty to yourself.

## Your Ruling Planet

It is not at all surprising that you are such an independent and inventive sign, because the discovery by Sir William Herschel in 1781 of your ruling planet, Uranus, coincided with new scientific discoveries and invention, and Uranus is always associated with change, independence and invention. Uranus has also been called the 'awakener of humanity to a new age'. It is certainly the influence of Uranus that makes you such a reforming, intellectual, progressive and often very scientific individual, but Saturn's influence may also act as a restraining force upon those rebellious and sometimes revolutionary qualities that can lead an Aquarian into trouble. It is almost certainly Saturn's influence that makes you appear quite aloof and detached at times.

In every star sign chapter, the 'typical' star sign personality has been discussed, but that is virtually impossible when a person can be as complex and non-conformist as you can! Uranus endows you with your sense of initiative and originality and its influence helps you to stride ahead and achieve your ideas. But Uranus is also responsible for your erratic, perverse, unpredictable and unconventional approach to life. Its influence can even make you anarchic and fanatical in your aims and ambitions, so it is important that you do not give way to the negative aspects of your ruling planet. You must find a way to go deeper within yourself and learn how to harness the power of Uranus, so that your nervous system remains in balance. This is because, astrologically, Uranus relates to the nervous system and to the electrical force flowing through the nerve channels.

In many ways it is wonderful to have Uranus as your ruling planet, for it seems to give you *carte blanche* to be independent, inventive and original in your self-expression, and to make the best possible use of your creative talents and abilities in every possible way. This ruling planet will also inspire you with reforming and pioneering ideas, and to speak out against injustice. Uranus relates to electricity, science and electronics, and its influence will help you to be extremely successful in the technological world in which we now live.

But you must learn to try harder to balance the negative with the positive, because then you truly will be able to turn your lofty ideals into existence – and enjoy a smoother journey through life.

## Your Ascendant and Moon Sign

As discussed in Chapter 1, in principle you will take on something of the personality of the sign that was rising when you were born. If your Ascendant is Aquarius, remember that the Uranus influence will be stronger too.

As an Aquarius with Aries rising you will be even more enthusiastic about realising idealistic visions but could be headstrong too; a Taurus Ascendant will help you to see the constructive and practical way forward, but hopefully not make you too stubborn; a Gemini ascendant will mean you need to organise yourself better and not be quite so 'free'; while Cancer rising will mean that you're far less detached emotionally and a lot more sentimental. With Leo rising you will be a real go-getter but could be financially extravagant; a Virgo Ascendant makes you less unpredictable and more analytical of yourself and others; Libra rising makes you charming, diplomatic and more intellectual; while Scorpio rising adds intensity to your emotions and a fairly invincible streak to your ambitions. A Sagittarius Ascendant adds to your confidence and optimism and gives you a wanderlust to see more of the world; a Capricorn Ascendant gives a pragmatic touch to your original approach to life; an Aquarius Ascendant could make you a real genius or just too cool, detached and unpredictable for your own good – so balance is definitely needed here; and, finally, a Pisces Ascendant will make you visionary and romantic, but you might also need to be more practical.

The Moon in your horoscope highlights both your emotions and your innermost needs. It will naturally have an effect on your star sign personality. As an Aquarius, with the Moon in Aries you will be an interesting blend of cool detachment and fiery emotions; a Taurus Moon will tone down your unpredictability and make you slow but sure in many ways; a Gemini Moon could mean you're somewhat scared of deep emotional ties but you will be brilliantly intellectual; and the Moon in Cancer makes you a sensitive humanitarian who needs lots of inner security. A Leo Moon makes you attractive and outgoing with lots of freedom-loving ways plus a deep desire to be loved and praised; the Moon in Virgo adds the need to be of service to your idealistically humanitarian ways; a Libra Moon could mean that your inner personality needs a perfect relationship while your outer personality seeks a free-and-easy involvement, so greater balance is the answer; while a Scorpio Moon will mean that burning passion may lie beneath the surface of your more detached exterior. A Sagittarius Moon means you will not only be unpredictable but even more adventurous and happy-go-lucky; a Capricorn Moon gives you more of a need for the traditional things in life; but an Aquarius Moon makes you even more unique, idealistic and unconventional in your ideas *and* your ideals; and, finally, a Pisces Moon makes you more intuitive and mystical. Your emotional needs also become more important.

## Accentuate the Positive and Reduce the Negative

In many ways you are amazingly positive, and incredibly curious about life and the future. But why can't you try to combine the idealistic and inventive characteristics of your personality with a little more realism, and try harder to show tenderness and understanding to the people with whom you share your personal life.

Be honest Aquarius – sometimes you are just too emotionally detached for words, which makes it almost impossible to know what you are thinking or feeling. Other people may think that you're simply not interested in them and unwittingly you may be upsetting them too. Try to concentrate more on the people and issues close at hand, instead of becoming so deeply involved in 'causes' that you lose sight of everything else.

Sometimes your head is a little too high up in the clouds, so that you visualise your image of Utopia but neglect to work out in practical terms just how to turn your dreams into realities. Don't let your energy be too scattered or you risk wasting a great deal of time on impractical issues. Remain idealistic – but resolve to be realistic too.

## Challenges and Obstructions

Although you usually hate to conform to any sort of rigid pattern, it is important to deal with any challenges and obstructions in a carefully thought out manner. Sometimes you have flashes of intuition which are quite brilliant in helping you to plan your moves, but you are also prone to unnecessary outbursts of temper which can lead you into trouble.

Unfortunately you can be incredibly dogmatic when you come up against a problem or conflict, and you seem to find it very difficult to see reason, especially with other people's views and opinions.

When you are under a great deal of pressure, your normal

aloofness can turn all too easily to erratic and irrational behaviour that becomes even more unpredictable, and some-times this also starts to make you even more fixed in your ideas and opinions, however unconventional they may be. Therefore it is really important for you to try and find a bal-ance between your sense of duty to the world and your sense of duty to yourself, and a meditation to help you release the stress that becomes bottled up inside you will be a real benefit.

## YOUR STAR SIGN MEDITATION TO HELP YOU CREATE A BETTER LIFE

☆ Sit comfortably on the floor in a cross-legged posi-tion (or, if this is not comfortable, on a chair).

☆ Because you are an Air sign, close your eyes and visualise yourself surrounded by limitless space.

☆ Imagine that you are looking as far and wide as you can, and also deep within yourself, to the infinite place that is your Inner Self. Feel the peace and freedom within you as you become more balanced on a mind, body and soul level.

☆ Allow your mind to be still, but don't worry if thoughts and ideas insist on coming in – just let them continue onwards into the limitless space all around you.

☆ Let yourself sink slowly into this meditative state for approximately 20 minutes, so that you have the time to let the peace and harmony flow through you.

Try to perform this meditation twice a day. You will become even more determined to put your humanitarian qualities to the best possible use, and to direct your idealism in a more positive manner. You will soon know intuitively when your 20 minutes are up. And when you next gaze up into the real space high above you, resolve that you will be less impersonal with your deepest feelings and perhaps just a little less unpredictable too.

## Balancing Your Inner and Outer Personality to Improve Your Relationships

If you are one of those typically unpredictable Aquarians, you must have realised by now that to achieve successful and fulfilling relationships it is important to let your feelings show a little more.

As a companion you are invariably extremely interesting, with the ability to converse on a myriad of fascinating subjects and a great sense of humour, but when it comes to a one-on-one relationship you seem to find it difficult to take things to a deeper level. It simply isn't enough to be able to theorise about love and passion in a general sense, or discuss them both intellectually for hours on end. Often you need to try harder to express your emotions with a more physical show of affection. Besides, if you're truly honest with your inner personality, and are not determined to be a loner, you would probably like to have a real soulmate just as much as any other sign. You are very successful at selflessly giving everything you have for a higher cause in which you believe — so why not make the need to create better relationships one of your Aquarian causes too!

## A Successful Career

Because you *are* so inventive, original, and innovative, you definitely have what it takes to be successful. But although you are often extremely talented, you are not always very ambitious in the accepted sense of the word. If you are determined to be more successful in your career you will always benefit by being sufficiently motivated by your own ideas or a cause to which you're prepared to dedicate yourself. Make sure that you have plenty of mental stimulation but try to accept that, although you hate routine, almost everything contains routine of one kind or another. When you are motivated *and* mentally inspired you will manage to cope with difficult deadlines and long hours without a problem.

To be even more successful you must learn to balance your individuality within your workplace with the commitment and ability to be an effective team player. Your multi-talented skills are invariably a bonus in your chosen career, but it is important not to scatter them in too many directions, or refuse to listen to constructive advice just because you consider that your ideas are best. And remember that too much Aquarian detachment can look like disinterest in your work — not a good idea if you want to become more successful!

# 13

# Pisces
# 19 February –
# 20 March

If you were born between 19 February and 20 March, you were born under the twelfth sign of the Zodiac, the sensitive and sympathetic, mystical and intuitive Pisces. You are the last, but definitely not the least, sign of the Zodiac. You are a Feminine, Mutable, Negative Sign, the last of the Water signs; your planetary ruler is Neptune, the Roman God of the Sea (Poseidon for the Greeks), and your planetary symbol is the Fish — two fishes swimming in opposite directions, upstream and down. In simple terms, you are gentle and kind, but you also have a tendency to drift with the tide and to be too much of a romantic dreamer.

If you're a typical Pisces, you will possess lots of creative ability, but often you find it hard to deal with running your life in a practical and organised way. Pisceans often need lecturing on their financial situation, because no matter how much they earn they always seem to find money a struggle by the end of the month. The same scenario will often apply to your romantic life, possibly as a result of your tendency to view the world through rose-coloured spectacles. Perhaps everything looks better with them on, but you simply cannot afford illusions if you want to have a more successful journey through life. Once you learn to sift the practical from the impractical (in every area of your life) you will be surprised how much easier everything will become.

Often you possess talents that for one reason or another you prefer not to develop. Perhaps it's a fear of rejection, so why don't you try to be a little more like an Aries and learn to thrive on challenges. Just because you are number 12 in the Zodiac it doesn't mean you have to come in last when they are handing out prizes for success.

You invariably 'feel' things more than all the other signs. But the trouble starts when you become too much of a chameleon, and begin to change your ideas and direction like the two fish that represent your sign. Don't simply 'go with the flow' or be quite so receptive to the influence of other people, and try harder to find more of a balance between your inner and outer nature.

## Your Ruling Planet

If you're a typical Pisces, perhaps it is not surprising that you possess those mythical 'rose-coloured spectacles'. It's almost too easy to blame it on your planetary ruler, although it's certainly true that Neptune endows you with both your inspirational and your somewhat unworldly qualities, and makes you dissatisfied if things do not turn out as you hoped. Neptune is associated with the psychic realm, imagination, intuition and dreams, but also with illusions, obsessions and hallucinations; it also rules alcohol and drugs.

However, the positive side of having Neptune as your planetary ruler is that it accentuates your creative talents and your idealism, your artistic sensitivity and your romanticism; and it can also produce an interest in mysticism. Unfortunately, the negative side of Neptune's influence can produce confusion, self-delusion and obsessions. It can make you gullible and prone to intangible fears and phobias, drug addiction, emotional instability and vacillation. It is often said that there is only a thin line between genius and madness. Therefore you must learn to be a wise Piscean who will maximise Neptune's potential in a positive way, so that you will be inspired to rise to greater heights and not be dragged down in any way.

The power of Neptune's influence is enormously beneficial, provided that you choose inspiration over illusion and escapism! But this should not be too difficult, and with your highly attuned intuition you will soon learn to avoid swimming in the wrong direction. By learning more about your sign, you will also discover the benefit of listening to your inner voice, and becoming more in touch and in balance with your innermost feelings and your deepest emotions. When you start to channel your innermost feelings upward into your conscious mind and allow your intuition to lead you in the best direction, you will also begin to create a more positive world, not only for yourself but also for other people.

Always remember that your ruling planet Neptune can help you to fulfil the magic of your particular dreams, but also that you must be the person in charge of ensuring that the dreams are practical. Vow to refrain from losing yourself in fantasy, and be happy that you have Neptune's influence to help you attain your highest aspirations in a positive and realistic way.

## *Your Ascendant and Moon Sign*

As discussed in Chapter 1, it is very likely that you will take on something of the personality of the sign that was rising when you were born. If your Ascendant is Pisces, remember that the Neptune influence will be stronger too.

As a Pisces with Aries rising you could still be a romantic dreamer, but you'll also be more of a go-getter; a Taurus Ascendant will help to balance your inspirational visions with greater determination and lashings of common sense; Gemini rising makes you more detached emotionally and you'll be great at putting across your creative ideas; while Cancer rising makes you extra sensitive and intuitive, but hopefully not too moody at the same time. A Leo Ascendant makes you far more extroverted than most Pisceans, and more self-confident; Virgo rising adds discipline and organisation to your list of virtues, but perhaps a little more self-criticism; a Libra Ascendant accentuates your caring ways, but might sometimes make you too vacillating; and Scorpio rising highlights your psychic abilities and makes you quite a power-player. A Sagittarius Ascendant makes you more fun-loving and energetic, and more freedom-loving; Capricorn rising could mean you're more of a workaholic than a dreamer; Aquarius rising will probably mean you're the most unpredictable Pisces of all; and, finally, if you have a Pisces

Ascendant you'll definitely be a romantic dreamer, but at least you'll be doubly intuitive!

The Moon in your horoscope highlights both your emotions and your innermost needs. It will naturally have an effect on your star sign personality. As a Pisces, with the Moon in Aries you will be impatient to express your innermost yearnings; the Moon in Taurus brings a decidedly practical note to almost everything you feel; a Gemini Moon will give you a need for lots of mental stimulation side by side with romance; while a Cancer Moon accentuates your ability to give lots of tender, loving care, and highlights your need for it too! The Moon in Leo will make you more dogmatic but perhaps even more romantic; a Virgo Moon could help you to avoid delusion by being more analytical; a Libra Moon will enhance your idealistic and compassionate ways, but you could be more indecisive; while the Moon in Scorpio adds intensity and sensuality to your more dreamy-eyed approach. A Sagittarius Moon adds an adventurous outlook to your more sensitive and subdued personality; a Capricorn Moon makes you much more serious about life than a typical Pisces; an Aquarian Moon makes you more detached emotionally and much more unconventional; and, lastly, a Pisces Moon means you're amazingly psychic and quite an old soul too!

## Accentuate the Positive and Reduce the Negative

A quote by Oliver Wendell Holmes particularly applies to the typical Pisces personality: 'A moment's insight is sometimes worth a life's experience'. It's wonderful to possess your insight, but it is necessary to make use of it too. Don't just file it away in your scrapbook of dreams. You don't have to stop being a dreamer, but it will be so much more positive if you try to turn the dreams into reality.

The positive side of Pisces makes you one of the most tender, mystical, sympathetic and compassionate people around. You have a scintillating sense of humour when you want to use it. But you can all too easily become melancholy and unrealistic. You are often an expert at calming other people, and helping them with their problems, and some of you possess a healing quality too. But you are not always expert at running your own life, especially when it comes to your financial situation! Always remember that although compassion and caring for other people is extremely worthwhile, this should not mean that you have no time to look after *yourself*. Learn to become more in touch with your Inner Self and to balance yourself on a real mind, body and soul level. This will help you to feel more secure so that you know exactly where you are going in your life.

## Challenges and Obstructions

Astrologically, Pisces relates to the twelfth house of the Zodiac, which in turn relates to the secrets that you keep hidden from the rest of the world and perhaps even from yourself. Challenges and obstructions are bound to create difficulties for a sensitive and gentle soul like you, and if you are a typical Pisces you will often do your best to escape from them, either by being exceedingly indecisive or by stalling for time. But this kind of behaviour will often make them a whole lot worse, especially if you are not prepared to discuss things with people who can give you constructive advice.

The twelfth house of the Zodiac is also known as the house of 'one's own undoing'. It is important for you to learn to deal a little better with practical issues and to differentiate between fantasy and reality so that you do not drift aimlessly when challenges or obstructions come along. Try to become more self-disciplined, and start to appreciate the benefits of structure and organisation in your daily life.

Don't get yourself into a flap over every little mishap, turning minor problems into major crises, or allow yourself to be influenced too much by other people when deep down you know the answers yourself. When you become more in touch with your Inner Self you will find that your intuition will become even greater, and no challenge or obstruction will seem to difficult to overcome.

## YOUR STAR SIGN MEDITATION TO HELP YOU CREATE A BETTER LIFE

☆ Sit comfortably on the floor in a cross-legged position (or, if this is not comfortable, on a chair).

☆ As you are a Water sign, close your eyes and visualise that you are sitting on the banks of a beautiful river. The sound of the water flowing by is very relaxing and if thoughts, ideas, impressions or sounds do insist on coming into your mind just let them drift on by.

☆ Let yourself flow freely with this river, the river of life, which is taking you in the right direction, towards what life has to offer.

☆ Allow yourself to sink slowly into a meditative state for approximately 20 minutes, so that you feel yourself taking in boundless love and releasing any feelings of doubt or negativity.

Try to perform this meditation twice a day. Looking within will be a journey to a wonderful world of enlightenment. It will help you to discover not only greater feelings of empathy towards others, but also a greater belief in your own contribution to the world.

And the next time you find yourself near a riverbank, stop for a few moments and watch the water flowing effortlessly by, taking any driftwood along with it without a problem. Affirm to yourself that *you* will find the best possible direction for *your* life, and always try to follow its path in a positive and realistic way.

## Balancing Your Inner and Outer Personality to Improve Your Relationships

Nine times out of ten Pisceans are more concerned with their romantic possibilities than about any other area of their lives. If you're a typical Pisces, romance appears to be the very breath of life itself! But you cannot always be a romantic dreamer.

Deep down you search for a true soulmate – someone who can relate to you completely in mind, body and spirit. But you must learn to balance your inner needs and desires with a more realistic approach so that your emotions and romantic fantasies don't lead you astray. Your ability to tune in intuitively to other people should be a fantastic bonus, but when it comes to relationships it seems to let you down.

If you're a typical Pisces perhaps the best advice is to listen to your head more often; don't just rely on your heart. Try to balance your mystical otherworldliness with a stronger dose of reality. In order to create better relationships, you need to have a good relationship with yourself. Perhaps you need to love and appreciate yourself more, deep inside, so that your emotions become stronger and don't lead you astray.

Affirm to yourself that you won't brood about the past, fantasise about the future, or let the present drift on by. Never let the ebb and flow of your emotions make you commit yourself to a relationship that you're not sure is right for you. When you become even more in touch with your Inner Self and tap the sources of your emotional strength you might be amazed just how strong you really are! Create a more balanced relationship with yourself — and the rest will surely come your way.

## A Successful Career

If you are a typical Pisces, one of the best ways for you to be more successful in your chosen career is to be much more positive about your talents and abilities. Try not to give way to those feelings of insecurity, inadequacy and self-doubt that often lie beneath the surface of your star sign personality. But make sure also that your goals do not belong in the realms of fantasy!

Many Pisceans tend to undervalue their creative talents, and demonstrate a rather touching humility, combined with an almost childlike delight and surprise when their ideals become achievements. However, you can be as successful as any other sign if you only take the time and trouble to go about things in the right way. Often it is your own lack of willpower or ability to organise yourself in a realistic way that holds you back. Sometimes you almost seem to be a person who wants success without putting in the necessary groundwork to achieve it, and yet if you are honest with yourself you will admit that you also have a deep need for recognition.

When you believe wholeheartedly in your work, you will become positively inspired and even more determined to fulfil your ambitions. This is why it is also extremely important for you to listen to your inner voice and be guided by what it tells you.

You are the last sign of the Zodiac, but you are definitely not the least! You will undoubtedly be able to achieve more success in your career once you have found your chosen direction and learned to stay on track.

# 14

# Astrological Advice for the New Millennium

New technological breakthroughs are achieved every day, some good and some not so good. Major changes are taking place all around us, and people are being affected in many different ways. But from the moment you are born, until it's time to leave this world, you will always be the same star sign, for that is something constant.

The more you learn, through the art of astrology, about how to understand yourself and other people in a more enlightened way, the easier you will find it to move ahead in the days and years to come. Astrology is a truly fascinating subject, for it will teach you something new every single day of your life. I hope this book will encourage you to learn more about it and that you also appreciate its benefits.

# Useful Addresses

Compiled with astrologer, Frank Clifford, author of *British Entertainers: the astrological profiles* (Flare Publications, 1997)

## *UK*

*The Astrological Association of Great Britain*, Unit 168, Lee Valley Technopark, Tottenham Hale, London N17 9LN. Tel: 020 8880 4848
*The Faculty of Astrological Studies*, 54 High Street, Orpington, Kent BR6 0JQ. Tel: 07000 790143
*The Mayo School of Astrology*, Alvana Gardens, Tregavethan, Cornwall TR4 9EN. Tel: 01872 560048
Principal: Jackie Hudson, D.M.S. Astrol.
*Equinox*, The Astrology Shop, 78 Neal Street, Covent Garden, London WC2H 9PA. Tel: 020 7497 1001. Fax: 020 7497 0344. Freephone: 0800 834 861. Website: www.astrology.co.uk and www.equinox.uk.com
For computerised charts and a wide range of books.
*Midheaven Bookshop*, 396 Caledonian Road, London N1 1DN. Tel: 020 7607 4133.

*Data Exchange*, Flare Publications, P.O. Box 10126, London NW3 7WD
For data about celebrities and contemporary figures. (Send s.a.e. for details.)

### Astrology Software

*Astrocalc*, 67 Peascroft Road, Hemel Hempstead, Herts HP3 8ER. Tel: 01442 251809
*Solar Fire*, c/o Roy Gillett, 32 Glynswood, Camberley, Surrey GU15 1HU. Tel/Fax: 01276 683898

### USA and Canada

*Equinox Astrology LLC*, 465 NE 181st Avenue, Suite 818, Portland, OR 97230. Tel: 1–888 283 0017. Fax: (503) 296 2069.

### Australia

*Equinox Astrology Pty. Ltd*, ACN 058 388 533, Level 1, 56 The Corso, Manly, NSW 2095. Tel: (02) 9475 0175. Fax: (02) 9475 0175.

### Astrology on the Net

http://www.urania.org
http://www.astrologer.com
(provides links to sites for astrology organisations, journals and events)
http://www.astrology-world.com
(articles and on-line debates on astrology, plus links and contact addresses)
http://www.flareUK.com
(website for new astrology books, plus discounts for popular astrology titles. Also gives information on astrology and palmistry consultations)

# Further Reading

Addey, John, *A New Study of Astrology*, The Urania Trust, 1996

Campion, Nick, *The Practical Astrologer*, Cinnabar Books, 1993

Cornelius, Geoffrey, Hyde, Maggie and Webster, Chris, *Astrology for Beginners*, Icon Books, 1995

Ebertin, Reinhold, *The Combination of Stellar Influences*, American Federation of Astrologers, 1972

Fenton, Sasha, *Reading the Future*, Piatkus, 1996

Gauquelin, Francoise, *The Psychology of the Planets*, ACS, 1982

Golder, Carole, *The Seductive Art of Astrology*, Henry Holt USA, 1989

Golder, Carole, *Love Lives*, Henry Holt USA, 1990

Golder, Carole, *Moon Signs for Lovers*, Henry Holt USA, 1992

Golder, Carole, *Carole Golder's Star Signs: How to Get in Touch with the Inner You*, Henry Holt, 1994

Golder, Carole, *Success Through The Stars: An Astrological Guide to Defining and Living a Satisfying Life*, Henry Holt USA, 1996 (out of print, only available through Equinox, The Astrology Shop and www.flareUK.com — see Useful Addresses)

Golder, Carole, *Your Stars At Work: Using the Power of Astrology* to Get Along and Get Ahead on the Job, Henry Holt USA, 1997

Goodman, Linda, Linda Goodman's Sun Signs, Pan Books, 1973

Greene, Liz and Sasportas, Howard, The Inner Planets, Weiser, 1993

Hand, Robert, Horoscope Symbols, Whitford Press, 1981

Hand, Robert, Planets in Transit, Whitford Press, 1976

Lyle, Felix and Aspland, Bryan, The Instant Astrologer Kit (book and CD-ROM), Piatkus, 1998

Pagan, Isobel, From Pioneer to Poet, Theosophical Publishing House, 1969

Rudhyar, Dane, The Astrology of Personality, Aurora Press, 1991

Sasportas, Howard, The Gods of Change – Pain, Crisis and the Transits of Uranus, Neptune and Pluto, Penguin Arkana, 1989

Sasportas, Howard, The Twelve Houses, Thorsons, 1985

Seymour, Percy, Astrology: The Evidence of Science, Penguin Arkana, 1990

Wright, Paul, Astrology in Action, Anodyne Books, 1988

Tompkins, Sue, Aspects in Astrology, Element, 1989

# Index